Austin Mardon   Kyra Droog

Alyssa Kulchisky   Theoren Tolsma

Mark Unruh

UNDERSTANDING MUSIC

An Interdisciplinary Study

Antarctic
Institute
of Canada

i

Typeset and cover by Josh Harnack

ISBN: 978-1-77369-148-0
Golden Meteorite Press
103 11919 82 St NW
Edmonton, AB T5B 2W3
www.goldenmeteoritepress.com

Antarctic
Institute
of Canada

TABLE OF CONTENTS

UNDERSTANDING MUSIC

An Interdisciplinary Study

INTRODUCTION

Music is a great blessing. It has the power to elevate and liberate us.
It sets people free to dream. It can unite us to sing with one voice.
Such is the value of music
- Nelson Mandela

From the time before our first breath to well after our final breath, music plays an inevitable and intrinsic part in our lives. Parents sing to their children while they are in the womb. Music marks the crossing of the stage at graduation. Hundreds of thousands of people gather together to celebrate a musician's live performance. Music plays in the car during road trips. Music celebrates our life once we are gone. This incredibly powerful mix of sounds is there to comfort us when we are sad, push us up when we are feeling down, and bring out our wild and excitable side when all we want is to scream a song at the sky. There is no shortage of ways to explain the power and importance of music in our lives, and no doubt that any list of moments in life that are marked by music will remain forever incomplete: music is a constant in every life.

A wide variety of definitions of music exist, particularly dependent on the style or type of music in question. This book will tackle a wide variety of music: everything from the first known forms of western art music to the latest songs telling stories of modern-day experiences. For our purposes, music will be: "a pattern of sounds made by musical instruments, voices, or computers, or a combination of these, intended to give pleasure to people listening to it" (Cambridge Dictionary, 2020). This all-encompassing definition means we aren't restricted to considering western art music or vocal music; instead, we can consider all forms of music that are intended to spark joy in listeners' hearts.

To truly understand music in an interdisciplinary way is first to understand the way music has grown and evolved based on human need. That said, in order to understand some of our discussions, we need to have a basic understanding of the history of music, but western art music particularly; when most people think about classical music, they are thinking of western art music. For this purpose, we will provide a brief overview of the important musical eras, musical forms, and other terms and concepts that will help you, our reader, navigate the coming sections of this book. To help with quick reference, we have also added a glossary of terms at the end of the book, which will help you should you become stuck on a specific term when we discuss it.

THE MUSICAL ERAS OF WESTERN ART MUSIC

Western art music encompasses a wide range of musical endeavours, and spans hundreds of thousands of years. In fact, "western art music extends from the great repertory of Gregorian chant, first assembled around the year 600 C.E., to compositions circulating electronically on the internet today" (Kerman & Tomlinson, 2015, p. 42). Even with this all-encompassing statement, it is truly difficult to understand how music emerged from single tone chants to the complicated symphonic masterpieces that exist today. To impart upon you, our readers, a basic understanding of how music changed and evolved throughout the years to keep up with the needs and desires of humankind, we will dive into the music of some of the most noted eras of western art music. Considering the history of music will help us understand some of the later sections in this book: much like the best way to understand how something works is to break it down to its most basic pieces and build it back up again, the best way to have a well-rounded appreciation for the complexities of music is to understand its basic composition.

The Middle Ages

The middle ages is the first period in the history of classical music whose composers can be identified by name. For centuries, following the Roman Empire's collapse, the main centres of learning in Western Europe had been the monasteries (Du Noyer, 2003, p. 255).

Much of Western life, including music, was determined by the church during the middle ages. With the sole exception being jongleurs, or court entertainers, all music was written by and performed in churches, and related to religious material. As Joseph Kerman and Gary Tomlinson explain: "music provides words with special emphasis, force, mystery, even magic. Throughout human history, this heightening by music has served the basic aim of religion: to bring humans into beneficial contact with unseen spirits, with deities, or with a single God" (2015, p. 44). It is for this reason, the connective aspect, that music played - and still plays - such an important part in religion and various religious gatherings.

It is important to note that this magic of music didn't exist solely within Christianity and Catholicism; many global religions utilize music in a variety of ways within their religious practice, helping them create deeper connections with their deities. When it comes to Christianity and Catholicism, however, much of the singing in which they would partake took the form of plainchant, or as it is better known, Gregorian chant. Named after St. Gregory I, Gregorian chant is known for being monophonic (single lined): a single melody without accompaniment. A wide variety of Gregorian chant genres exist, and as time went on, they became more ornate. Typical Gregorian chant wasn't based on the major/minor modes we use today; instead, it was based off of the medieval modes, where scales were arranged around D, E, F, or G (Kerman & Tomlinson, 2015, p. 46). This is one reason that modern listeners recognize Gregorian chant as sounding "different" than regular music: it's fundamental basis is different from much of the music we listen to, which is arranged around a C scale. Specific songs were chanted at various masses, including the Kyrie, the Gloria, the Credo, the Sanctus, the Benedictus, and the Agnus Dei.

As the middle ages progressed, so did the purpose of music in everyday lives. It was at this time that the popularity of court songs began to spread, and so the music of the troubadour was introduced. Troubadours were "one of a class of lyric poets and poet-musicians often of nightly rank who flourished from the 11th to the end of the 13th century, chiefly in the south of France and the north of Italy, and whose major theme was courtly love" (Merriam-Webster, 2020). This music was played predominantly for royalty, who could commission songs or poems from specific troubadours. Interestingly, "some of these noble songwriters penned the words only, leaving the music to be composed by jongleurs" (Kerman & Tomlinson, 2015, p. 49). Today, the idea of one person creating the lyrics while another creates the song itself, to be heard for the first time in front of a live audience, seems absurd, but in the middle ages, the partnership of troubadour and jongleur appeared to be mutually beneficial.

Even at the time of the troubadour songs were still simple and contained only a single melody. It wasn't until later in Medieval Europe that the very fabric of music changed when polyphony was introduced. Polyphony consists of "the simultaneous combination of two or more melodies" (Kerman & Tomlinson, 2015, p. 52), and fundamentally changed the way music existed, both in terms of Gregorian chant and music moving forward in history. The earliest known type of polyphonic music was called organum, and "consisted of two melodic lines moving simultaneously note against note" (Encyclopaedia Britannica, 2020). This form of embellishment to traditional Gregorian chant brought a whole new world of options to plainchant, and "flourished at the Cathedral of Notre Dame in Paris" (Kerman & Tomlinson, 2015, p. 52) which housed composers such as Pérotin, sometimes known as Pérotin the Great. Interestingly, and in direct opposition to the way many songs are written today, "early organum [...] was, it seems, spontaneously produced by specially trained singers before being committed to manuscript" (Encyclopaedia Britannica, 2020). In this way, organum was produced by composing out loud as opposed to composing on a page.

In essence, it was during the time of Medieval Europe that the basics of song emerged: moving slowly from a single monophonic chant into a more ornate polyphonic song. At the same time, music outside the church also evolved as the power of the music traded hands between the troubadours and jongleurs. It is without question, however, that the introduction of polyphony to religious chant set musical history on a course that would only grow more and more ornate, complicated, and fascinating.

The Renaissance

The rich interchange of ideas in Europe, as well as political, economic, and religious events in the period 1400 - 1600 led to major changes in styles of composing, methods of disseminating music, new musical genres, and the development of musical instruments (Arkenberg, 2002).

The Renaissance, or the rebirth as it is often known, was a time of large and important change in Europe. These changes occurred in all aspects of life, but the changes in music were large and profound, creating ripples that affected the ways that music existed throughout the world. While music was still traditionally utilized for the church, it also began to be enjoyed without reprieve outside of the church, a movement which encouraged creativity and imagination regarding music's true limits.

Many changes to music were initiated from changes to the music of the church. During the Middle Ages, we noted that church masses moved from being monophonic to polyphonic; interestingly, "the fifteenth century also saw the beginning of composed homophony - that is, music in a harmonic, chordal texture" (Kerman & Tomlinson, 2015, p. 61). Homophony can be seen through another change to church masses: the creation of the ordinary of the mass, in which five specific texts were written for the choir. These five texts include "the Kyrie, a simple prayer; the Gloria, a long hymn; the Credo, a recital of the Christian's list of beliefs; the Sanctus, another shorter hymn; and the Agnus Dei, another simple prayer" (Kerman & Tomlinson, 2015, p. 63). Interestingly, these five standardized texts live on in a variety of forms during many masses today.

During the Renaissance, music not only changed in terms of homophony - the ways in which music was written also changed. Music during this period saw a rise in imitation, which added a new layer to musical experiences. As musicologists Joseph Kerman and Gary Tomlinson write:

> A first voice begins with a motive designed to fit the words being set. Soon other voices enter; one by one, singing the same motive and words, but at different pitch levels; meanwhile the earlier voices continue with new melodies that complement the later voices. Each voice has a genuinely melodic quality, none is mere accompaniment or filler, and none predominates for very long (2015, p. 64).

Alongside this imitation came acapella; performances with no instruments, only voice. While many of us modern-day folk will recognize acapella from shows like Glee and Pitch Perfect, acapella lived predominantly in the church during the Renaissance, and gave life to religious choirs. Instead of using external instruments and additional musicians, the music lived within each person, and they came together to share that with their audience.

Outside of the church, music was also changing. The introduction of the madrigal, a "short composition set to a one-stanza poem - typically a love poem, with rapid turnover of ideas and images. Ideally, it is sung by one singer per part, in an intimate setting" (Kerman & Tomlinson, 2015, p. 72), brought a whole new form of music to the world. The key phrase to focus on here is 'intimate setting' because it is here we note a change in physical setting for music. In the church, masses consist of a large audience, yet for the madrigal, small and intimate audiences were a fundamental requirement: the madrigal wasn't meant for large audiences. Madrigals were often accompanied by instruments like the lute, and saw great success in the Renaissance, as ideas about the way the world worked began to fundamentally change. We must remember that the Renaissance was a time of exploration where, for the first time since the middle ages, art and music began to have a great impact and truly matter to people again.

Though classical music didn't make a true introduction until the early Baroque era, it is important to note that it was during the Renaissance that composers began experimenting with the opposite of acapella: music without voice. During this time, predominant instruments included the lute, the flute, and the harp, though the harpsichord and organ had recently been invented; many of the instruments we typically associate with classical music hadn't yet been brought to the table. "Purely instrumental music included consort music for recorder or viol and other instruments, and dances for various ensembles" (Lumen Learning, 2020). Because classical music was, at this time, still in its infancy, its true power had yet to be revealed.

Much like in other aspects of Renaissance life, music was focused on the idea of enlightenment; of questioning current boundaries and opening up new doors. The Renaissance was the first time in which printed music was available (Lumen Learning, 2020), and was one of the first times that music outside of the church and court was encouraged and enjoyed. By taking this step to essentially remove musical power from church and court, music became more accessible to the general public, leading to the playing of music at public events such as dances. This change in access to and purpose of music fundamentally changed the way that music would be enjoyed for thousands of years to come.

The Baroque Period

Absolutism and science were two of the most vital currents that defined life in the seventeenth and early eighteenth centuries. The result was an interesting dualism that can be traced throughout Baroque art: pomp and extravagance on one hand, system and calculation on the other. The same dualism can be traced in Baroque music (Kerman & Tomlinson, 2015, p. 99).

Though each of the musical eras we discuss in this book have had a large impact on musical history, the Baroque era itself truly changed the fabric of music because, in it, the purpose of music and the ways in which music was created were fundamentally revisited. Interestingly, the common definition of Baroque comes from Jean-Jacques Rousseau: "music is that in which harmony is confused, charged with modulations and dissonances, in which the melody is harsh and little natural, intonation difficult and the movement constrained" (Buelow, 1993, p. 1). It was during the Baroque period when classical music truly came into being, when music truly was removed from the power of the church and court, and when musical exploration achieved new heights. Because the Baroque era, which spans from 1600 to 1750, covers such immense ground, it is typically split into the early Baroque period, and the late Baroque period, each of which have unique musical styles and tendencies for us to explore.

In order to truly understand the great strides that music took during this age, we also need to understand the ways in which the world itself changed. During the Baroque period, calculus, the telescope, the microscope, and the theory of gravity were discovered; discoveries which lead to a greater understanding about the world we live in. These scientific discoveries actually played into musical discovery as well. As Kerman & Tomlinson note, "people began to think about ordinary matters in a new way, influenced by the newly acquired habits of scientific experimentation and proof" (2015, p. 98). One of these ordinary matters that was reconsidered was music, and from that reconsideration came a whole new way of creating, appreciating, and sharing music.

Early Baroque

> The genre of music theatre most typical of Western classical music emerged during the first decade of the seventeenth century, initially as an entertainment for the Florentine aristocracy. It then spread to Mantua, Rome, and other Italian cities, before its arrival at the Teatro San Cassiano in Venice, the first operatic venue dependent on a fee-paying general public (Du Noyer, 2003, p. 258).

One of the most important ways in which music evolved during the early Baroque period was through the creation and dissemination of the opera. As Kerman & Tomlinson note: "Opera - drama presented in music, with the characters singing instead of speaking - is often called the most characteristic art form of the Baroque period" (2015, p. 83). This new way of telling a story through music, with the addition of actors, exploded in popularity both in Florence, where it originated, and across the world. Not only that: operas combined many of the things that had been reborn in the Renaissance whose importance continued throughout the Baroque period: art, dance, expression, storytelling, and music. Much like typical classical music, many operas were created using a system of musical and storytelling formulas. Two of the most recognizable standards in operatic music are the recitative and the aria.

Recitative is, as Du Noyer notes, "devised to make [opera singers'] utterances sound lifelike. Based on the contemporary style of how the poems of Ancient Greece were performed, the recitative style preserved the natural speech rhythms of the words and used them melodically over a simple chordal accompaniment" (2003, p. 258). Using the recitative allowed for everyday speech, or the portions of the opera that were not sung, to have a rhythmic aspect to them, making them sound like music, regardless of whether or not they were. Du Noyer also noted that the recitative mirrored typical Ancient Greek spoken poetry, which provided a connection to the history of in many cases, the times in which the stories operas told were set.

Aria, on the other hand, is "an extended piece for solo singer that has much more musical elaboration and coherence than a passage of recitative. The vocal part is more melodic, the rhythm is more consistent, the meter clearer, and typically the accompaniment includes the entire orchestra" (Kerman & Tomlinson, 2015, p. 84). The aria is an important musical moment in the opera, typically used to portray a specific emotion or share a reaction to a drastic change in a character. When a typical person thinks of an opera singer, the singing they imagine - loud, expressive, and covering multiple pitches within the same note - is often in the aria style.

Within opera, but also within other music typical of the early Baroque era, emerged another trend that the early Baroque era came to be known by: the basso continuo. The introduction of new and different instruments to both classical music and the opera opened many doors at this point in history, and because each new instrument was suited to a new purpose, many new aspects to music were continually utilized as composers established an instrument's best use. Instruments like the harpsichord and organ were often used for the basso continuo which "reinforces the bass line but also adds chords continuously to go with it [...] [and] has the double effect of clarifying the harmony and making the texture bind or jell (Kerman & Tomlinson, 2015, p. 82 - 83). In essence, these instruments played a supporting role as the basso continuo helped strengthen and add interest and complexity to the baseline of a composition.

Instrumental music wasn't leading the scene in the early Baroque period like opera was; instead, it was utilized like the Renaissance, in a social setting to encourage dancing and similar celebration. That said, not many great strides were made in the form of instrumental music during this time, as forms were relatively similar when utilized for the purpose of dances and other celebrations. The fugue, however, is a typical Baroque musical form which "uses only one theme throughout - like a single extended point of imitation - and often treats that theme with great contrapuntal ingenuity and learning" (Kerman & Tomlinson, 2015, p. 91). Much like modern jazz, variations on the theme were improvised on the spot, so it took musicians with a special ear for melody and harmony to be great at managing expectations of the fugue.

The early Baroque period was a time of learning and exploration; moving into a time where dance, song, and storytelling became one. Opera opened many doors, to both new forms of musical endeavours and new endeavours within existing musical forms. The recitative and aria both affected opera music directly, but also played a part in music outside of the opera, as the forms could transfer to other types of music. The basso continuo changed the impact a baseline had in a composition, which thereby changed the method of composition and the traditional way of thinking about a composition. All of these additions to music culminated throughout the early Baroque period and led to even further discovery and intrigue in the late Baroque era.

Late Baroque

> The eighteenth century was a great age for the crafts [...] - composing music was also regarded as a craft. The Romantic idea of the composer - the lonely genius working over each masterpiece as a long labor of love expressing an individual personality - was still far in the future. Baroque composers were more likely to think of themselves as servants with masters to satisfy. They were artisans with jobs, rather than artists with a calling. They produced on demand to fill a particular requirement (Kerman & Tomlinson, 2015, p. 105).

One of the biggest reasons for the differentiation between the early and late Baroque periods is the extent of musical change that occurred between 1700 and 1750, which is what we know as the late Baroque period. Interestingly, much of the music we know as Baroque music is actually late Baroque music, as it was during this time that composers began to truly understand these new methods of music making and find ways to add their personal touch to them. Two composers in particular, whom we will discuss shortly, left their mark on the late Baroque era in such a way that their names are often synonymous with the term Baroque music.

Before we discuss specific composers, however, we need to be aware of some of the fundamental changes in music itself during the late Baroque period. There are many ways in which late Baroque music stands out from every other musical era; namely, the dramatic ways in which dynamic changes were utilized. Dynamics would change from the softest piano to the loudest fortissimo in the blink of an eye to create intense and dramatic effect; gradual build-ups and slowdowns were reasonably infrequent. By utilizing this effect, composers brought unexpectedness to the table in a way that hadn't often been utilized prior.

If late Baroque era music was a painting, it would be extravagant, with many colours, shapes, and sizes present. One of the highest values of music in this era was its ornamentation; that is, "the addition of fast notes and vocal effects (such as trills) to a melody, making it more florid and impressive. Ornamentation is typically improvised in the music of all cultures, and in Western music is often written out" (Kerman & Tomlinson, 2015, p. 427). Much like the ornamentation that formulates typical jazz music, taking the written music and making it into something more extravagant was a fundamentally appreciated aspect of late Baroque music. Ornamentation is one of the ways in which historians are able to decree whether music is considered late Baroque style, since it played such a prevalent part of music at the time.

Earlier in this section, we explained that orchestral music didn't come into its prime until the late Baroque era. Orchestral music emerged on scene with the concerto and concerto grosso. We will be talking in further detail about the aspects of the concerto in a later section, but thought it important to provide a brief outline of the concerto here as well. As Kerman and Tomlinson explain: "The basic idea underlying these genres is contrast between an orchestra and a soloist (in the concerto) or a small group of soloists (in the concerto grosso) (2015, p. 115). In essence, the concerto is what you yourselves have likely witnessed in a concert hall: the orchestra playing as a whole before the soloist emerges and plays atop the orchestra's sound.

Because of the introduction of the concerto and concerto grosso, the fabric of instrumental music changed: instead of short dance forms, audiences wanted to hear longer, more intricate pieces of music that exemplified both soloists and the whole orchestra. When compared to the past instrumental music, Russell Torrance notes that: "as time went on, purely instrumental music became more prominent but the idea of separating players into groups persevered — and developed. What if you have groups of different sizes? Instant loud and soft parts. What if the smaller group could be given more intricate, "showy" parts?" (2019). And not only did composers split players into groups; they also created the idea of musical movements or, "a self-contained section of music that is part of a larger work; movements in books can be compared to chapters in a book" (Kerman & Tomlinson, 2015, p. 116). Movements were then tied together in specific forms to create full concertos.

There were a few composers in particular whose names are recognizable through the ages that reigned during the late Baroque period. First, we must introduce Arcangelo Corelli (1653 - 1713), who is "the composer most readily associated with the development of instrumental music at the turn of the eighteenth century" (DuNoyer, 2003, p. 260). Interestingly, one of the reasons the violin is as popular in a symphony orchestra as it is today is because Corelli utilized it with such prominence throughout his compositions. Antonio Vivaldi (1678 - 1741) and Johann Sebastian Bach (1685 - 1750) both took on the challenge of the concerto and expanded it to become something new and exciting each time. Vivaldi, for example, wrote hundreds of concertos, making each different from the next; each time, creating something new and exciting for his listeners to hear. Bach composed the Brandenburg Concerto, which is one of the most popular concertos from this period. In short, there are many incredible composers that we have to thank for their dedication and focus on taking instrumental music and making it something fascinating for listeners and performers alike.

One final important note about late Baroque music regards the orchestral dance music of the time. As was the norm, this music was split into movements. These movements were often structured in specific ways, and in time, were given names. For example, the minuet is "a simple dance in triple time at moderate tempo" (Kerman & Tomlinson, 2015, p. 132), and a gigue is "danced by couples in formal ballet style" (Encyclopaedia Britannica, 2020). The arrangement of the musics in the suite, or complete dance composition, depended on the composer, but was typically in the style of minuet, trio, minuet/gigue, with a musical theme continuing through the entire suite. The reason these dance suites are important to us as we learn about musical history is because of their organization: symphonies reached back to the way suites were organized and adapted a similar form of organization much later on in history. This adaptation goes to show that though popular composers of the time may not have known it, they were blazing the trail for future musical compositions.

The Classical Era

One of the Enlightenment's principal thinkers, Jean-Jaques Rousseau, was concerned with making music accessible to a wider audience, and defined it as "the art of inventing tunes and accompanying them with suitable harmonies (DuNoyer, 2003, p. 262).

The Enlightenment, or the classical period as it is often known, brought about yet another great change to the musical stage. Music itself was placed squarely on the main stage, particularly thanks to Thomas Jefferson's "life, liberty, and the pursuit of happiness." After all, music and the arts provide happiness even in times of deepest despair. In addition, the classical orchestra was introduced, changing the fundamental tone colour, or sound, of music itself. Not only did the classical period introduce the symphony to the world; it also helped teach listeners to understand and follow classical forms, providing the audience with a sense of confidence and understanding as they slowly learned to anticipate where the music would take them next.

The symphony, which we will discuss in more detail further on, truly defined the classical era, as it opened a new door to how audiences could experience music. The classical era was one of the concert hall: where people would purchase tickets to gather together in large groups in a single space to hear an orchestra play. Though this had obviously been occurring throughout history, the concert hall and the purpose and glory of the symphony orchestra really came to light in the classical era. In essence, the symphony brought large groups of people together to celebrate their love for music, thereby encouraging connection and celebration in a new and intriguing manner.

Yet, the symphony wasn't the only type of music that shot to the top during the classical era. The classical concerto, a take on the Baroque concerto, also became extremely popular, in part because it was so different from the Baroque concerto; now, it had a specific form - double-exposition form - which it followed, providing composers what constituted a script for composition and allowing listeners to create and manage expectations for what would appear in a classical concerto and in what order. Though double-exposition form is similar to that of sonata form, which we will discuss later when we look at the symphony in detail, it is also more expansive than sonata form.

Another important musical form in the classical era was the string quartet. A string quartet is "an ensemble of four solo strings, traditionally two violins, viola, and cello. Through achievements of Haydn, Mozart, and Beethoven, it has come to symbolise the loftiest form of discourse in instrumental music (BBC Music Magazine, 2016). Because of the quartet structure, string quartets were often present in smaller, more intimate performances; whereas thousands of people would attend a symphony performance, string quartet performances would often have a much smaller audience. An important note about string quartets is that they function without a conductor; instead, they listen closely to each other as they adjust according to the others' playing. "This interplay has been aptly compared to the art of cultivated conversation - witty, sensitive, always ready with a perfectly turned phrase - that was especially prized in eighteenth century salons" (Kerman & Tomlinson, 2015, p. 188). String quartets introduced chamber music, or smaller concert experiences with two to nine instruments, to the world.

The classical era truly was a time of musical discovery in that so many new and exciting musical forms emerged. From the symphony to chamber music, music had become more accessible to everyone, and was beginning to branch off into genres that would help everyone find something they loved and appreciated. From the opera, which was still running strong, to a small string quartet, the variety of music in the classical era was unmatched by any other era in history.

The Romantic Era

Musical romanticism was marked by emphasis on originality and individuality, personal emotional expression, and freedom and experimentation of form. Ludwig van Beethoven and Franz Schubert bridged the classical and romantic periods, for while their formal music techniques were basically classical, their music's intensely personal feeling and their use of programmatic elements provided an important model for 19th century romantic composers (Encyclopaedia Britannica, 2020).

As Paul DuNoyer notes: "above all, the romantic period was a literary age" (2003, p. 264). Much inspiration for romantic music came from the stories that the music was telling, and the ambition of these stories and how they could be told overtook composers, leading to some of the most complicated and fascinating musical endeavours of the time. It was during the romantic era that books like Frankenstein were being written, and with that came an interest in the supernatural in writing, art, and music.

It is important to note that the romantic era and the modern idea of what is romantic, are very different. The romantic era wasn't focused on couples massages and Valentines Day; instead, it was about personal expression and creativity - finding new ways to express feelings and emotions and share them with the world. Historically, the term romantic was used to describe language that flourished and embellished and made things beautiful, such as tales of chivalry in the Renaissance. "In the eighteenth century, the semantic field of the word 'romantic' in common English usage had expanded to include the picturesque, the fanciful and the fantastic with not altogether positive connotations" (Seyhan, 2009). It was during the romantic era that this focus on beauty, individuality, and emotion returned, particularly thanks to program music.

Program music "is a term for instrumental music written in association with a poem, a story, or some literary source - or even just a highly suggestive word or two" (Kerman & Tomlinson, 2015, p. 228). Imagine taking your favourite book or short story and composing music that you think would fit perfectly alongside the story: that is what program music is. In the third section of this book, we will be exploring Hector Berlioz's Symphonie Fantastique, which is romantic program music at its best and most bizarre. For now, we need to understand that the focus of most instrumental music at this time was on telling stories.

And yet it wasn't only instrumental music that focused on telling stories; the romantic era's "most distinctive genre in the field of chamber music was the song with piano accompaniment" (DuNoyer, 2003, p. 261). The German Lied, or song with piano accompaniment, often told a variety of stories in a cycle. "Late 18th and early 19th century romanticism gave great impetus to serious popular poetry, and many poems of such masters as Goethe were set by Lied composers" (Encyclopaedia Britannica, 2020). One of the most popular Lied composers of the time was Franz Schubert, who composed over 600 Lieder during his time. We will be looking in-depth at the Lied and doing a case study of Schubert's Lied "the Erolkönig" in the third section of this book.

In addition to the popularity of smaller, more intimate compositions, the romantic era also had a focus on large, grandiose compositions unlike any other. These compositions occurred in both symphonic and operatic form, and challenged the former constraints of how long a symphonic or operatic work could be. "For example, Hector Berlioz's symphony Romeo and Juliet of 1839 lasts for nearly an hour and a half [whereas] a typical Haydn symphony lasts twenty minutes (Kerman & Tomlinson, 2015, p. 230). On the opera side of things, there is no better example of a grandiose composition than Richard Wagner's The Nibelung's Ring, which "goes on for four evenings with a huge orchestra including specially invented instruments, a cast of thirty, and fifteen separate stages" (Kerman & Tomlinson, 2015, p. 230). Compositions of such magnitude encouraged composers to step outside their comfort zones to create new, ambitious, and exciting compositions of their own.

Another new musical form that emerged during the romantic era was that of the character piece. Character pieces are fascinating creatures in that they are short compositions whose fundamental purpose is to describe a certain character, be it a person, an emotion, an object, or something else entirely. As Kerman & Tomlinson note: "each [character piece] conveys an intense, distinct emotion - an emotion often hinted at by an imaginative title supplied by the composer (2015, p. 243). For the most part, these character pieces consisted of piano music alone, in the form of piano miniatures.

The romantic era took to the edges of the spectrum: some pieces were small, short, and emotional, and some pieces were grandiose, long, and extravagant. These polar opposites were nothing like each other but, interestingly enough, did feed into each other as each focused on telling stories and encouraging audiences to feel a specific way. This focus on feeling had its roots in every musical era, but truly came to flourish during the romantic era. The romantic era also continued the tradition of expanding the limits of music; pushing the boundaries to see what new and interesting ways music could be composed, played, and understood, a tradition that continues on into the modernist period.

Twentieth Century

By the turn of the twentieth century, western classical music seemed to have reached a crisis in language. Tonality had become enfeebled by its own progressive tendency, via increasing chromaticism, towards subtler and more complex forms of expression. European society had become similarly enervated by the familiar comforts of a bourgeois existence (DuNoyer, 2003, p. 268).

As one can inevitably imagine, Western art music has changed fundamentally in the last one hundred years. Much like with the aforementioned musical eras, in order to provide a brief description of the most important of these changes, a large amount of fascinating and important history will unfortunately be missing. That said, there are a few extremely important aspects of twentieth century music that we need to understand in order to move forward in section five to one particularly fascinating musical form that became popularized in the twentieth century: the American Musical.

To discuss twentieth century music, however, is to introduce a variety of schools of thought that had a large impact on the music of the time. The first era we will discuss is the modernist era, which "has been a period of turbulent change in music style and taste. Many modern 'art-music' composers have explored untraditional sounds and based their music on rhythm, texture, and tone color instead of the more traditional aspects of melody and harmony" (Western Michigan University, n.d.). In short, modernism was equivalent to anti-traditionalism in that composers attempted to find new ways to present their music that worked against the typical musical traditions. Korman & Tomlinson note that: "the chief composers associated with the modernist movement in this early phase were Claude Debussy, Arnold Schoenberg, and Igot Stravinsky" (2015, p. 302).

Within early modernism is where impressionism can be found, a musical style that Claude Debussy in particular initiated. "Impressionism can be seen as a reaction against the rhetoric of romanticism, disrupting the forward motion of standard harmonic progressions" (Encyclopaedia Britannica, 2020). Impressionism led to a new type of music which exemplified melodies that lacked direction, and sounds that broke all the pre-existing musical rules. Debussy's Clouds is one popular example of impressionistic music.

Impressionism then led to expressionism, which took music one step further away from the aforementioned pre-existing musical rules. With high levels of dissonance, distorted melodies and harmonies, and lots of dynamic contrast, expressionistic music "exploited extreme states, extending all the way to hysteria, nightmare, even insanity" (Kerman &

Tomlinson, 2015, p. 320). One of the most recognizable expressionistic images is Edvard Munch's The Scream: when we think of the painting, we start to understand the ways in which expressionistic music took form. In short, "expressionist composers poured intense emotional expression into their music and explored the subconscious mind" (BBC Bitesize, 2020).

Now, we've discussed consonance and dissonance often in the previous paragraphs, but never stopped to take the time to understand them. According to the Encyclopaedia Britannica, consonance and dissonance are "the impression of stability and repose (consonance) in relation to the impression of tension or clash (dissonance) experienced by a listener when certain combinations of tones or notes are sounded together" (2020). In essence, music that is consonant sounds stable and comforting, but music that is dissonant sounds unstable and tense. Think about it this way: when you're watching a movie, you always know when the villain is on-screen, because you can hear and feel the music become more tense. This is because dissonant themes are common in villain themes when it comes to soundtrack music. In essence, consonance and dissonance are like the yin and yang of music: the balance of stability and instability.

Of all the music we have discussed thus far, American music has not played a part, predominantly because "America has no rich tradition of classical music" (Kerman & Tomlinson, 2015, p. 330). It wasn't until the twentieth century that America truly came onto the classical music scene. Charles Ives (1874 - 1954) was "[America's] first important nationalist composer. But he was also more than that: a true American original, a man with amazingly radical ideas about music, and a bold experimenter with musical materials." (Kerman & Tomlinson, 2015, p. 330). Ives wholly embraced the ideas of expressionism and impressionism, writing with dissonance, and utilizing quarter tones instead of half tones when composing for the piano. Though much of Ives music wasn't widely discovered until his late years, he is unquestionably the first American modernist, who led the way for many more to come.

If we make a substantial jump in history, remembering that we are looking at a brief overview and not a deep dive into Western Art Music, we enter a whole new genre of music: soundtrack music. The first film with synchronized sound was released in 1927, adding another aspect to the complex mix of audio and visual that is a film. King Kong (1933) was the first film to have an original score written for it; before that time, any music written for film had been written after the fact, and was performed live in the theatre alongside the film itself. From this monumental moment, the film and television music industry has grown widely, to include such historic themes such as Raiders of the Lost Ark (1981), Star Wars (1977), and Hawaii Five-0 (1968 - 1980; 2010 - Present).

After film music came electronic music. As the Western University of Michigan website explains:

> Modern technological advances (especially mass media) have caused rapid changes in musical style, and expanded our knowledge of music from other cultures, further accelerating changes in musical taste while providing a wider range of music to listeners, composers and performers. Today, new musical ideas and styles can be introduced almost instantly, allowing large-scale trends to change in months or years, instead of decades. Computer-based technologies, synthesized sounds, and new recording techniques continually add new dimensions to today's music (2020).

The advent of digital technology opened up new doors to music, even insofar as to allow individuals who have no musical background and play no musical instruments to compose their own music from their homes. The era of electronic music, which we still exist in today, has provided composers exciting new opportunities; at the same time, it has enforced the perceived antiquity of the traditional symphony and symphonic live performance. As history continues, music continues to change quickly as new trends are taken on across the world.

Western art music has existed for thousands of years, and has changed in virtually every aspect during its existence. From the invention of new musical instruments and new musical forms to the change in focus regarding what stories compositions should tell and how long they should be, the history of western art music is long, intricate, and fascinating. Our understanding of the briefest outline of this history will, as we mentioned, help us understand the ways in which music 'grew up' and came to be the phenomenon it is today. This history will also help us decipher some of the musical forms, which we will discuss in the next section.

A BRIEF INTRODUCTION
TO MUSICAL FORM

As we delve into the meat and potatoes of this book, we will be speaking in detail about a few important musical forms. That said, it is important for us to have a brief understanding of these musical forms as we move forward, so we can have a well-rounded appreciation for the ways in which these different forms affect us on varying levels. From the Baroque concerto to the American musical, these musical forms have all existed in our lives one way or another, and would absolutely be recognized within the first few bars of their most popular songs. With that, let's learn about the history, construction, and applications of the following musical forms.

Concerto/Concerto Grosso

> Indeed, the word concerto comes from the Latin word concertare, to contend - an origin that accurately indicates a sort of contest between solo and orchestra. This contest pits the brilliance of the soloist or soloists against the relative power and stability of the orchestra. Contrast comes to these genres naturally (Kerman & Tomlinson, 2015, p. 115).

The reason we begin with the concerto is because the concerto is essentially an early version of the symphony; to understand the symphony is to understand the basic layout of the concerto. We'll remember from our Baroque section that the concerto is "a large composition for orchestra and solo instrument (Kerman & Tomlinson, 2015, p. 424). The concerto was truly the beginning of large compositions for orchestra, which is why it is the most logical place to begin our introduction to musical form. Being that this form was brand new during the Baroque era, it makes sense that as composers continued to explore the form, a method of identifying the form would become available.

The concerto was one of the first musical forms that utilized movements, or a "self-contained section of music that is part of a larger work" (Kerman & Tomlinson, 2015, p. 116). One of the easiest ways to identify the movements of a concerto is to consider one of the most famous and well-known concertos: Vivaldi's Four Seasons. There are four distinct movements that match each of the four seasons: Spring, Summer, Winter, and Fall. Each of these movements is distinct from the other, following different forms. There are a variety of forms, but we will discuss two of the most common forms below.

Ritornello form "is characterised by a recurring A section in between new sections of music, and is often described as 'ABACA', where the A section contains a distinctive theme. Importantly, the recurring A section is rarely an identical repeat of the first time we hear it" (MyTutor, 2019). In essence, this means that there is a recurring theme throughout the form, wherein the theme is played (A), a new theme is introduced (B), the original theme is reintroduced (A), a third theme is introduced (C), and the original theme returns to end the movement (A). The emphasis on contrast in ritornello form is high, as you will note: there are only three themes, but the original theme is in direct contrast with the other two themes that are introduced.

The second common concerto form that we will discuss is variation form: "a form in which a single melodic unit is repeated with harmonic, rhythmic, dynamic, or timbral changes" (Kerman & Tomlinson, 2015, p. 430). Variation form has a much less distinct organization than ritornello form; instead, it allows the composer more freedom in their composition. One of the defining features of variation form is repetition, like ritornello form, but it's often the repetition of a strong bass line, commonly known as the basso ostinato. This bass line will repeat throughout the movement, often playing either beneath or above a soloist. As we mentioned, variation form can be more difficult to comprehend when it comes to organization, since there is no true organization of the form, but it can easily be recognized through its strong and unrelenting bass line.

Another important aspect of the concerto is the cadenza. The cadenza is an "unaccompanied bravura passage introduced at or near the close of a movement of a composition and serving as a brilliant climax, particularly in the solo concerti of a virtuoso character" (Encyclopaedia Britannica, 2020). If we consider the ending of Bach's Brandenburg Concerto No. 5, we realize exactly how important the cadenza can be, as it truly sets a dramatic and exciting ending to the final movement of a concerto. This fast and brilliant virtuoso truly envelopes the style of the concerto, and is one of the easiest ways for even the non-musical to pick a concerto out of a crowd.

Being that concertos predated the symphony, there is a logical connection between the two, particularly when it comes to organization and form. As we move into our discussion of the symphony, it will become clear how aspects of the concerto are glaringly obvious in the symphony, and how symphonic composers returned to ideas brought about in the concerto to help bring both bustling activity and organization to their symphonic masterpieces.

The Symphony

As concerts became more and more frequent, people felt a need for a song genre that made an effective, substantial focus for these occasions. Symphonies answered the need - and in turn required more variety and flexibility of sound than anything orchestras of the early eighteenth century could provide. The symphony spurred a major technical development within music, the evolution of the Classical orchestra (Kerman & Tomlinson, 2015, p. 161).

Much like the concerto, the symphony is organized into movements; in typical symphonies, there are four movements broken down into the following:

Movement 1: Fast/Moderate speed, often sonata form
Movement 2: Slow speed, often in variation of sonata form or rondo form
Movement 3: Moderate speed, often a dance form like minuet/trio
Movement 4: Fast movement in either sonata or rondo form

Sonata form, often the form of the opening movement in a symphony, is easily recognized by its three-part structure. "The basic elements of sonata form are three: exposition, development, and recapitulation, in which the musical subject matter is stated, explored or expanded, and restated" (Encyclopaedia Britannica, 2020). The three elements of sonata form are often notated with ABA'.

The exposition, (A) "is a large, diverse section of music in which the basic material of the movement is presented" (Kerman & Tomlinson, 2015, p. 163). In the first movement, this is the time at which the main theme of the work is presented, first in the main key, and then again in the secondary key. Next, a new theme in the secondary key is introduced and explored, before the closing theme; in essence, a grandiose lead up to the end of the exposition.

The development (B), takes all of the themes and keys in the exposition and breaks them down so that they can be built up in new ways: "That is, themes or fragments of themes may appear in new keys; they may be combined to form apparently new melodies; they may be played against each other as counterpoint, or countermelody" (Encyclopaedia Britannica, 2020). This section encourages dissonance and restlessness, as it appears the melody is broken, both in notation and in key. At the end of the development, the retransition occurs, welcoming the original theme in its original key back to the composition.

The recapitulation (A') essentially repeats the exposition section with minor changes; notably, the exposition is played solely in the second key, not the original key. In some cases, both the exposition and the development can be repeated. The recapitulation gives composers a sense of freedom in the changes they can make to the exposition while still providing their listeners recognizable content, ensuring that as they continue through the symphony, they will be able to recognize the theme in a variety of keys and methods of organization. The end of the recapitulation marks the end of the first symphonic movement.

The second movement of a symphony is what most people would consider the sad movement of the symphony: it's slow speed and often introspective tune lend itself to a more emotional ride than any other symphony movement. This movement is often presented either in rondo form - which we will discuss in terms of the fourth movement - or a version of sonata form, which we just discussed. In general, "the movement gradually gains momentum and tension, taking you to a turbulent and emotional high before masterfully gliding back down" (Bennet, 2017).

The third movement of a symphony is a large transition from the second, in almost every aspect. Where the second movement is slow and introspective, the third movement is quick and engaging, with a strong beat. There is a reason the third movement is often known as the dance movement; mostly because the third movement is typically presented in either scherzo or minuet form.

Minuet form, the more common choice for the third movement of a symphony, was one of the most common dance forms in the seventeenth and eighteenth centuries, making it a logical choice for a fast and exciting symphonic movement. Much like sonata form, minuet form also consists of three sections: a minuet, a trio, and then a minuet. Kerman & Tomlinson (2015, p. 173) described minuet form in the following diagram:

Minuet	Trio	Minuet
A	B	A
|: a :||:b :|	|: c :||: d :|	ab

In essence, this means that the overall third movement would resemble AABBCCDDAB, if put into a more readable form. Remember that in music, |: means repeat once; that should help your comprehension of the above diagram. The minuet is formed somewhat like sonata form; within a minuet, the theme is introduced (a), replayed (a), played in an altered form (b), and then replayed in that same altered form (b). Of course, the composition is much more complicated than this, but for our purposes, we need to understand only the basic functions of minuet form.

The trio's "primary job is to establish melodic and harmonic contrast" (Open Music Theory, 2018). The trio functions much like the sonata's development, wherein it contrasts the original melody and harmony in a variety of ways, before the minuet returns for a triumphant and dramatic return to end the third symphonic movement.

Scherzo form, the second most popular option for the third symphonic movement, is interesting in itself. An invention of Beethoven's genius, the scherzo is often known as the joke movement, based on the fact that scherzo means joke in Italian. "Unlike the rather stately minuet, originally a dance of the aristocracy, the scherzo in rapid 3/4 time was replete with elements of surprise in dynamics and orchestration" (Encyclopaedia Britannica, 2020). The scherzo is still a dance movement, yet it is more abrupt and changing than the typically smooth minuet. This alternate form also, once again, offers composers more freedom from requirement, as the technical requirements to meet scherzo form were fairly lax. That said, the movement is still, like the minuet, quick, fantastic, and with a strong beat that is easy for dancers to follow.

The fourth and final movement of a traditional symphony often follows one of two forms: sonata form, which we have previously discussed, or rondo form. Rondo form is a popular conclusion form because of its speed and energy, which lend themselves well to the exciting end of a symphony. Kerman & Tomlinson (2015), explain the outline of rondo form:

> A rondo begins with a full-fledged tune (A) and comes back to it after episodes (B, C, etc.) serving as spacers between its appearances. Longer rondo tunes may return in shortened form. For example, if A is the favourite |: a :|: b a' :| pattern of the time, the recurrence of A throughout the rondo may present a b a', b a', or even a alone. There is always enough of the tune for the listener to recognize it (p. 177).

Essentially, the rondo begins with a tune, and continues to loop back to the original tune, much like in sonata form. The main difference is that there are less 'rules' about how the original tune returns in rondo form; whereas in sonata form, much of the organization is mapped out, there is more compositional freedom present in rondo form. Rondos can also be present in a wide variety of schemes; that is, the organization of the sections. For example, a rondo could be ABACA or ABACADA: there are many options available for the composer to choose from.

The symphony is one of the most important and well-recognized forms of classical music in existence, and our understanding of it will not only assist us in our everyday lives, but will also help us during our deep dive into the fifth movement of Hector Berlioz's Symphonie Fantastique in section three. In short, the symphony is an extremely influential form of classical music, and being able to break it down into its sections and analyze how it is put together not only makes for extremely interesting learning, but also prepares you to consider musical content in new and intriguing ways.

The Lied

The text of a Lied [plural, Lieder] is usually a Romantic poem of some merit (at least in the composer's estimation). Hence, although we need to understand the words of almost any vocal music, with the Lied we should also try to appreciate how the poem's words and meanings fit together as poetry. The art of the Leid depends on the sensitivity of the composer's response to the poetic imagery and feeling (Kerman & Tomlinson, 2015, p. 234).

One of the most popular forms of romantic miniature music, the Lied is a curious and fascinating musical form that has been popular for an extended period of time. It is important for us, in the context of this book, to understand the Lied because in section three, we will be doing a case study of Schubert's Erlkönig, which is one of his most recognizable Lieds. To provide context for the upcoming discussion, we must understand a brief history of the Lied and some important aspects that make up a Lied.

As Kerman & Tomlinson's above quote explains, a Lied is based on a poem. Whether that is a poem written by the composer, a poem from thousands of years ago, or somewhere in-between does not matter: what matters is a Lied has a vocal aspect as well as a classical aspect. The classical aspect of a Lied predominantly consisted of piano accompaniment; it's important to remember that Lieder are more of an intimate musical form, meaning they were intended for smaller audiences and smaller scale performances than something like a symphony. As Kerman & Tomlinson note, "a Lied is nearly always accompanied by piano alone, and the accompaniment contributes significantly to the artistic effect. Indeed, the pianist becomes more of a discreet partner to the singer than a mere accompanist" (2015, p. 233).

Though the Lied has been around since the twelfth and thirteenth centuries, the most recognizable Lieder today came from nineteenth century composers such as Franz Schubert, Robert Schumann, Johannes Brahms, and Hugo Wolf (Encyclopaedia Britannica, 2020). Many Lieds in this era were based on romantic poetry; in the case we will consider in section three, by Johannes Wolfgang von Goethe, "a Romantic and a Classical poet, novelist, playwright, naturalist, and philosopher, and a favourite source of texts for many generations of Lied composers" (Kerman & Tomlinson, 2015, p. 234).

There aren't particular forms that Lieds follow; after all, it all depends on the poem the Lied is based on, and the Lieder composer. That said, "a Lied may be either through-composed or strophic, i.e., repeating the music for each new stanza of the poem" (Encyclopaedia Britannica, 2020). Because of the unique focus of the Lied, there are few rules for its composition, making it a fascinating and interesting musical form to study and understand.

Program Music and the Program Symphony

> Program music for orchestra grew up naturally in opera overtures, for even in the eighteenth century it was seen that an overture might gain special interest if it referred to moods or ideas in the opera to come by citing (or, rather, forecasting) some of its themes (Kerman & Tomlinson, 2015, p. 247).

Program music is a unique musical form whose history lends itself nicely to an understanding of the roots of the American musical, which we will be discussing next. Program music itself is defined as "instrumental music that carries some extramusical meaning, some 'program' of literary idea, legend, scenic description, or personal drama" (Encyclopaedia Britannica, 2020). In short, it is music that tells a story. The description may sound all-encompassing, but in reality, program music is allocated to a special place in musical form particularly because of the program symphony.

Program symphonies are "entire symphonies with programs spelled out movement by movement" (Kerman & Tomlinson, 2015, p. 249). One of the most famous program symphonies, and the one which we will analyze in depth as a case study for section three, is that of Hector Berlioz's Symphonie Fantastique. In this program symphony, Berlioz tells a specific story, going so far as to spell it out in pamphlets which were handed to his audience as they entered the chamber to listen to the symphony. Now, the program symphony follows many - if not all - of the 'rules' that the traditional symphony sets out, and we already have a basic understanding of the way symphonic form exists. That said, the biggest difference with the program symphony is that it is difficult to consider it a technical form: "it has been stated that the concept of program music does not represent a genre in itself, but rather is present in varying degrees in different works of music. Only in the so-called romantic [...] is the program an essential concept, and even there it leaves its mark on much music commonly considered pure or absolute" (Encyclopaedia Britannica, 2020). In short, the program symphony is more abstract than the typical musical genre in that it encompasses a wider variety of expression.

Another important example of the program symphony was that of Felix Mendelssohn's A Midsummer Night's Dream, which told the story of the Shakespeare play by the same name. This is different from Berlioz's symphony in that the story the symphony told was pre-existing, whereas Berlioz wrote the story of his Symphonie Fantastique himself. It is more typical for program symphonies to be based on existing stories, partially because of the ease in understanding the story without words. It goes without saying however, that both forms of the program symphony were incredibly successful and detailed in their musical storytelling.

As we move forward from the program symphony, which we will indeed discuss again, we realize that the program symphony came after most opera, which could be considered program music, yet with lyrics instead of being solely orchestral. Recognizing the part that opera played in the creation of programmatic music, including the program symphony, will be of great benefit to us, particularly as we move into the final musical form we will discuss: the American musical.

The American Musical

The rise of the musical in the 1920s and 1930s was closely tied to the great outpouring of popular songs in this era. It was truly a golden age for song (Kerman & Tomlinson, 201, p. 398).

The history of the American musical is vast and deep, to the point where many books could be (and have been) written with the sole focus on its roots. With the fact in our mind that we only need a brief overview of this history in order to critically understand section five's deep dive into Lin Manuel Miranda's Hamilton, we also must understand that the American musical was born of a deep and meaningful history, much of which we are unable to touch on in such a small section.

Before we jump into the American musical, however, we must remind ourselves that America did not have a deep tradition of western art music, and that as America came into its own, it began forming its own musical roots and history. Jazz music in particular played an important part in the growth and expansion of the American musical, though that's not at all to say it was the only musical form that influenced the ways in which the American musical exists. Interestingly enough, "it was around 1910 that the American popular theatre picked up its characteristic accent. It was a musical accent and came from jazz. Although Boraodway did not employ actual jazz, it swiftly assimilated jazz syncopation and swing" (Kerman & Tomlinson, 2015, p. 398).

This was the era of the musical comedy. At this time, consumers wanted to hear American stories with American locations, and American ideals, complete with dance and song. In a sense, this age of musical comedy was similar to the opera, but instead of opera singing, featured talking and non-opera musicale. From this age, which was known as "the golden age for song" (Kerman & Tomlinson, 2015, p. 398), a new sophistication emerged in the 1940s with the introduction of shows like Oklahoma! And West Side Story to the Broadway stage. West Side Story is fascinating in itself because it was essentially the first Broadway play of its kind to utilize vernacular in the way it does: "we see the cultivated tradition reaching out to the vernacular - but in a genre defined by the vernacular" (Kerman & Tomlinson, 2015, p. 399).

After West Side Story came a wide variety of Broadway shows, as wide and exciting as anyone could have imagined. From Hair to Grease to Phantom of the Opera, hundreds of Broadway shows have met with unfettered success. Interestingly enough, much like the opera and the symphony, there is a typical structure that American musicals follow, extremely similar to that of the novel: setting the scene, introducing the characters, introducing the conflict, rising action, climax, falling action, resolution, and conclusion. Outside of this structure, there is very little musical structure common throughout American musicals, outside of the tradition of having an orchestra playing the background or foreground music in the pit near the front of the stage.

As you will see in the fifth section, Hamilton challenges some of these traditional structures; for example, the entire two hour and forty minute show is nearly all presented as a rap. That said, Hamilton is quintessentially an American musical for a multitude of reasons: telling the story of the birth of America itself, presenting the storyline in accordance to the typical novel structure, and providing catchy and exciting tunes to encourage the audience to fully engage with their Broadway experience. The American musical has come far from its roots, and will unquestionably continue to grow as time goes on.

NAVIGATING THIS BOOK

Now that we have covered a brief history of western art music, as well as a brief introduction to the musical forms you will need to know and understand, we can move forward into what can be considered the 'meat and potatoes' of this book: an interdisciplinary study of music. The book is structured to move from the most to least empirical methods of studying music: from science to linguistics and communication, to philosophy and politics. By considering music from a wide variety of fields of study, we are able to take into account all of its different aspects and the way it is intended to affect us physically, mentally, and emotionally.

Just as we started this book by breaking down the history of western art music, we will begin the first section of this book by breaking down exactly what constitutes music: the fundamental physics of how music is created and how we are able to comprehend it. From there, we will move forth to discuss the biological reactions of the body to music, and the psychology behind our comprehension of music. After that, we will dive into linguistics and consider music as a language: how does it speak to us? Then, we will consider music from a communication lens and establish some of the key ways in which music communicates specific feelings to us through the theory of musical semiotics. The next section will introduce us to some key philosophical thinkers and their studies regarding music and the ways it impacts our everyday lives. Finally, we will consider some of the political implications of music: how it is utilized for a variety of purposes, and how its utilization in political senses can change or influence musical artists, composers, and the general population. A glossary of terms will be provided after the book's conclusion, to assist you, our readers, in understanding terms that may have previously been unfamiliar to you. That said, it is now time to learn about music itself, by learning about the fundamental fabric of sound: physics.

SECTION 1: SCIENCE

CHAPTER 1:
THE PHYSICS OF
SOUND AND MUSIC

Before we can begin to understand the many ways in which music impacts our lives on a daily basis, we must distill the truly complex concept of music down into its most basic forms. In order to properly discuss music, we need to understand what music is, to a deeper understanding than just it being the sound coming from a musical instrument or the rumbling of our vocal chords as we talk. By understanding the physics of the most basic element of music - sound - we will be able to set out some base definitions and understandings that will carry through the remainder of this book. Have no fear, for we will not be delving deeply into complicated equations nor difficult concepts; instead, we will be providing you with a brief overview of the most basic physics required to understand how sound works, how we measure it, and what impact it has on our everyday lives.

SOUND AND SOUND WAVES

According to David Young and Shane Stadler, "sound is a longitudinal wave that is created by a vibrating object, such as a guitar string, the human vocal cords, or the diaphragm of a loudspeaker. Moreover, sound can be created or transmitted only in a medium, such as a gas, liquid, or solid" (2018, p. 439). According to this physics-based definition, sound is a wave; more precisely, a periodic wave, which occurs over and over again by the source. To understand this concept, think about the sound a flute makes when a flutist holds a single note for an extended period of time, or when an opera singer holds their final note in all of its glory. Though a single note is being held, the note is not flat; in fact, there are slight changes in pitch in a cyclical up and down motion, known as vibrato. Vibrato is an excellent way for us to understand the waves that make up sound, particularly since we just defined sound as a wave created by a vibrating object.

It is important to note that there are a wide variety of wave shapes, many of which play important parts in our lives. Though we will only be talking specifically about longitudinal waves, understanding that longitudinal waves aren't the only type of wave is important because it helps shape the way we understand the universe around us. The following images depict some of the types of waves: the longitudinal wave, which we will be discussing, and the square wave and saw wave, which are examples of other waves existing in our daily lives.

Our definition of sound also noted that sound must be transmitted through a medium: it cannot exist in a vacuum. Kiona Smith-Strickland explains this phenomenon:

> When an object moves — whether it's a vibrating guitar string or an exploding firecracker — it pushes on the air molecules closest to it. Those displaced molecules bump into their neighbors, and then those displaced molecules bump into their neighbors. The motion travels through the air as a wave. When the wave reaches your ear, you perceive it as sound (2015).

Without molecules to move, sound waves are unable to exist. There have been many debates surrounding what this means for sound in space, and whether sound waves can exist in space's endless vacuum. Interestingly enough, space isn't a perfect vacuum: there are objects in space for sound to move from (think asteroids and other matter floating in space), and on average, there are 10 protons per cubic meter (L. Droog, personal communication, July 19 2020). For our purposes, we need to understand the ways in which sound is created, and how it moves through the air before reaching our ears.

Sound Frequency

There are many terms used when discussing sound that we must also understand in order to move forward with our discussion about interdisciplinary ways to understand music. The first of these terms is frequency. Young and Stadler (2018) define frequency as "the number of cycles per second that passes by a given location" (440). Frequency is measured in hertz. An excellent way to understand frequency is to use one of Young and Stadler's examples: the different sounds that occur when you press different numbers while dialing a phone number. Each number sounds different because it occurs on a different frequency, with some smaller waves having a higher number of cycles per second, and some larger waves having a lower number of cycles per second (Young & Stadler, 2018, p. 440 - 441). Frequency is inversely related to wavelength, ergo the longer the wavelength is, the lower the frequency will be. This concept is similar in music; as we will learn, different notes will create different sound waves, which will reach the ear at a different frequency, thereby sending different electron impulses to the brain, causing us to hear each note separately.

The frequency of a sound affects more than just the multitude of available notes we have in our musical toolbox. In fact, there are frequencies of sounds that are either too high or too low for the human ear to hear, which causes different biological reactions to the sounds. We will discuss the biological reactions in the next chapter, but for now, we need to understand that sound waves below a certain frequency (<20Hz) are inaudible, as are sound waves above a certain frequency (20,000Hz). When a person blows on a dog whistle, for example, they cannot hear the sound it emits but their dogs can, because dogs can hear sounds at frequencies higher than humans. As Young and Stadler explain:

> Frequency is an objective property of a sound wave because frequency can be measured with an electronic frequency counter. A listener's perception of frequency, however, is subjective. The brain interprets the frequency detected by the ear primarily in terms of the subjective quality called pitch. A pure tone with a large (high) frequency is interpreted as a high-pitched sound, while a pure tone with a small (low) frequency is interpreted as a low-pitched sound (2018, p. 441).

When we think about music in this sense, we realize that each instrument plays at a unique pitch; whereas a flute is more high-pitched, a tuba is more low-pitched. There are cases in which playing a musical note that is below the frequency a human ear can be beneficial and have a specific musical effect, which we will discuss in section three.

Sound Intensity

As you likely already know, while sound is capable of being calming and soothing, it is also capable of great destruction; not by its lyrics or musical form, but by its intensity. Sonic booms, for example, are waves of sound that are capable of breaking glass and sending buildings crumbling to the ground. Even the cliché example of an opera singer breaking a glass with their loud, high-pitched voice counts under the category of sound intensity.

So what is sound intensity? Mathematically speaking, sound intensity is "the sound power (P) that passes perpendicularly through a surface divided by the area (A) of that surface" (Young & Stadler, 2018, p. 446); the equation for which would resemble I = PA where I is the sound intensity, P is the sound power, and A is the surface area. Peak intensity occurs when the power that passes through the surface is perpendicular (L. Droog, personal communication, July 19, 2020). What we need to understand from this equation are the parts that make up sound intensity, and how it can be measured when required.

We must also understand the threshold of hearing, which relates directly to sound intensity. We spoke earlier about the fact that there were some sounds we could hear and some that we cannot; the human ear is only able to detect sounds within a specific spectrum. The threshold of hearing is "the smallest sound intensity that the human ear can detect" (Young & Stadler, 2018, p. 447). The intensity of the sound we hear, then, relates to our threshold of hearing because anything outside our threshold of hearing can be classified as a higher intensity than sounds inside our threshold of hearing. This concept will be important as we move into the biology of sound in the next chapter.

Understanding how to compare sound intensity is also important, particularly if we were to think about comparing the intensity of sounds in our everyday lives. Decibels are the unit of measurement used to compare sound intensities; they allow us to understand which sounds are more or less intense than others. For example, if we were to compare the decibels of music coming from our phone speakers to the loudness of a jet engine starting, we would likely establish that the jet engine will have higher decibels than the music our phone is playing. MyHealth

Alberta (2018) put together a helpful chart that explains which sounds are typically at which decibels:

Noise	Average decibels (dB)
Leaves rustling, soft music, whisper	30
Average home noise	40
Normal conversation, background music	60
Office noise, inside car at 60 mph	70
Vacuum cleaner, average radio	75
Heavy traffic, window air conditioner, noisy restaurant, power lawn mower	*80–89 (sounds above 85 dB are harmful)*
Subway, shouted conversation	90-95
Boom box, ATV, motorcycle	96-100
School dance	101-105
Chainsaw, leaf blower, snowmobile	106-115
Sports crowd, rock concert, loud symphony	120-129
Stock car races	130
Gun shot, siren at 100 feet	140

For reference, the bel scale is logarithmic, and with each increase, the intensity increases tenfold. So moving from 1bel to 2bel means the sound is ten times more intense. Increasing from 2bel to 3bel means the sound is 100 times more intense (L. Droog, personal communication, July 19, 2020). Interestingly, one bel is equal to ten decibels. With that in mind, when we look through this chart, we can consider the sounds we encounter in our everyday lives and how they may be affecting our hearing. For example, if we worked at a stock car race three times a week, we would be exposed to higher decibel levels more often than if we worked in a quiet office.

At this point, an important distinction needs to be made between increasing sound intensity and the loudness of a sound. As Young & Stadler note:

When a sound wave reaches a listener's ear, the sound is interpreted by the brain as loud or soft, depending on the intensity of the wave. Greater intensities give rise to louder sounds. However, the relation between intensity and loudness is not a simple proportionality, because doubling the intensity does not double the loudness (2018, p. 449).

In order to understand this principle, let's put it into practice following some of Young & Stadler's examples. As they explain: "to double the loudness of a sound, the intensity must be increased by more than a factor of two" (2018, p. 450). Thus, to make a sound louder, the intensity must be doubled at a minimum. On the other hand, "hearing tests have revealed that a one-decibel change in the intensity level corresponds to approximately the smallest change in loudness that an average listener with normal hearing can detect" (Young & Stadler, 2018, p. 449). So, it is easier to increase the intensity of a sound than it is to increase the loudness of a sound simply because whereas small changes can be detectable in the intensity of a sound, it takes a lot larger a change to detect an increase in the loudness of a sound.

THE PHYSICS OF MUSIC

Now that we have a basic understanding of the physics of sound, we can move into some of the ways physics applies to music specifically. The physics of sound are fascinating as a base for our understanding, but the physics of the musical instruments we use to create sound are even more interesting and exciting, as they follow many different and intriguing rules as music is created. As Glenn Elert explains: "the distinction between music and noise is mathematical form. Music is ordered sound. Noise is disordered sound" (2020). Now, we get to delve into some of this ordered sound and explain how it is created and ordered in such a mesmerising and beautiful way.

Standing Waves:

As we discussed earlier, sound consists of longitudinal waves that oscillate, or move back and forth in the same direction that the wave itself is moving (Somara, 2016). Many instruments, including string, wind, and brass instruments, don't use longitudinal waves; instead, they consist of standing waves. Standing waves are "waves which appear to be oscillating vertically without travelling horizontally. [Standing waves are] created from waves with identical frequency and amplitude interfering with one another while travelling in opposite directions" (Khan Academy, 2020). Without going into too much unnecessary detail, standing waves appear to be standing still, relative to its surroundings, yet still have a changing amplitude.

"Standing waves with different frequencies correspond to different musical notes" (Somara, 2020). For example, when a guitar string is strummed, you can physically see the string vibrating, but it looks like the string isn't actually moving: as if the vibration is occurring in a tube. Similarly, when a trumpet is played, the air molecules are doing the same thing: causing the air to vibrate, but not in a large wave pattern. The frequency at which the air or string molecules vibrate at dictates the musical note that emerges from the instrument.

The effect of standing waves depends on a few key ideas; specifically, the nodes of the standing wave and the interference they receive. Nodes are "positions on a standing wave where the wave stays in a fixed position overtime because of destructive interference" (Khan Academy, 2020). For example, if you tied one end of a skipping rope to a pole and began to flick the end of the skipping rope up and down, you would see the waves leaving your side of the skipping rope in the direction of the pole. Once those waves reached the pole, however, they would attempt to return to their source, which can cause the peaks of the outgoing wave to line up with the troughs of the incoming wave, cancelling out the wave and causing the skipping rope to become straight. This is what destructive interference looks like; in music, destructive interference causes silence because "when two opposite waveforms are added, they cancel out, leaving silence" (Hollis, 2017). On the opposite hand, the outgoing and returning waves could have peaks and troughs that match together, causing larger matching waves, which would be called constructive interference, and would lead to a sound.

The final important aspect of standing waves that we need to understand is that of overtones. As Benjamin Hollis explains: "overtones are the other frequencies besides the fundamental that exist in musical instruments. Instruments of different shapes and actions produce different overtones. The overtones combine to form the characteristic sound of the instrument" (Hollis, 2017). Since each instrument has a different and distinct overtone, the sounds they make are different. For example, when a flute and a clarinet play the same note, the sound that emerges from their instrument are tonally the same, but the sound is different because each instrument has a different overtone.

Vibration, Pitch, and Tone:

We have fundamentally established that sound is created through vibrations. The specific type of vibration, and what part of the instrument is vibrating, determines the specific sound it will make, and what tone it will create. For example, consider a bell. When a bell is rung or struck, the entire bell vibrates. When a violin is played, the string of the violin vibrates, and reverb occurs through the inside of the instrument, but the instrument itself does not vibrate. When a glockenspiel is played, it resonates at different frequencies depending on which key is hit. We can classify the types of instruments based on which parts of the instrument vibrate in specific ways, but this classification does not always hold up to the more traditional instrument classification methods; for example, not all woodwinds have reeds that vibrate, and not all percussion instruments have a stretched membrane that vibrates.

The natural vibration of an instrument helps to determine its pitch. As Glen Elert explains, "the human auditory system perceives the fundamental frequency of a musical note as the characteristic pitch of that note. The amplitudes of the overtones relative to the fundamental give the note its quality or timbre" (2020). So, then, the human ear denotes frequency as pitch when it comes to musical instruments. The Encyclopaedia Britannica defines pitch as:

> In music, [the] position of a single sound in the complete range of sound. Sounds are higher or lower in pitch according to the frequency of vibration of the sound waves producing them. A high frequency (e.g., 880 Hz) is perceived as high pitch and a low frequency (e.g., 55 Hz) as a low pitch (2020).

In essence, this means that our ear and brain detect the frequency of a sound and equate the frequency to a pitch, which we then associate with an instrument. For example, a flute would be a high pitch instrument, and a tuba or bassoon would be a low-pitch instrument.

A musical tone can have a wide variety of definitions, but for the purposes of this explanation, we will refer to a musical tone as the Encyclopaedia Britannica does: "sound that can be recognized by its regularity of vibration" (2020). A musical tone is often characterized by a variety of ways, including pitch, loudness, length, quality, and/or colour. "A simple tone has only one frequency, although its intensity may vary. A complex tone consists of two or more simple tones, called overtones" (Encyclopaedia Britannica, 2020). The use of simple and complex tones is essentially interchangeable with the terms monotonic and polytonic; referring to pure or single tones and multiple or a mixture of tones, respectively.

> Music in its simplest form is monotonic; that is, composed only of pure tones. Monotonic music is dull and lifeless like a 1990s ringtone (worse than that even); like a 1970s digital watch alarm (now we're talking); like an oscillating circuit attached to a speaker built by a college student in an introductory physics class (so primitive). Real music, however, is polytonic — a mixture of pure tones played together in a manner that sounds harmonious (Elert, 2020).

A symphony orchestra, for example, would play polytonic music simply because there are multiple instruments playing multiple notes at the same time. Much of the music we will discuss in this book will be polytonic or complex music because it will involve many aspects, from instruments to voice, and anything and everything in between.

Conclusion

Boiled down, the basis of everything upon this earth is, in essence, directly related to physics. Learning about the physics of sound and music allow us to move forward in this book with a basic idea of the ways in which sound and music are created, categorized, and understood, knowledge which will help us better comprehend the coming topics as we work our way through this book. As we move through the coming chapters, remembering the basics of sound and sound waves will allow us to understand the physical ways in which sound and music impact us, and understanding some basic musical terms in reference to their physics definitions and applications will provide us with a perfect reference board as we continue our journey towards truly understanding music.

CHAPTER 2:
THE CHEMISTRY OF
SOUND AND MUSIC

Of the four sciences that we are observing - physics, biology, chemistry, psychology - chemistry seems to be the least applicable, on its face at least, to music. If chemistry and music relate, it is by way of the brain. Increased knowledge of neurochemistry in recent decades has drastically broadened the way we think about our brains in relation to the rest of our bodies and the outside world. The study of neurochemistry can also provide a new and crucial entry point for understanding not only why we like the music that we do, but also why music has been such an important part of human life for thousands of years.

Our discussion of chemistry and music begins and ends with an exploration of neurotransmitters. There are three neurotransmitters released in the brain that play a crucial role in the way scientists understand the pleasure that we receive from listening to music: oxytocin, dopamine, and serotonin. First, we might ask, what are neurotransmitters? Neurotransmitters are a type of chemical messenger that sends signals by way of synaptic transmission. They have an essential function in the way in which one neuron or neural cell communicates with another, and are therefore vital for our brains to function.

The first, and the most well-researched, neurochemical related to our discussion is oxytocin, which is a neurotransmitter most commonly known as the "love hormone" and, although it is thought to be instrumental in our human relationships, is also observed in a wider range of functions. More aptly, clinical psychologist Carol Rinkleib Ellison called oxytocin the "hormone of attachment" (Livescience,

2013). This hormone is "produced in the hypothalamus of the brain and released by the posterior pituitary gland" and "facilitates pair-bonding and social interactions" (Livescience, 2014; Lane et al. 2013). As a more specific function, oxytocin is known to have a definitive reproductive effect, especially in women. As behavioral neuroscientist Larry Young stated, studies have shown that oxytocin was "first recognized for its role in the birth process, and also in nursing" (Livescience, 2015). When released in the brain, oxytocin prepares the female body for the changes that are necessary to deliver and support a healthy baby, which includes enhancing the relational bond between the child and the mother. More generally, oxytocin is known to be correlated with feelings of safety, security, and openness to vulnerability in social situations. Lane et al. show that oxytocin "increases people's willingness to share their emotions" through verbal communication, which increases bonding between two individuals and strengthens one's ability to create further relationships (2013). Lastly, oxytocin is related to our memory and learning when it comes to social interaction. Hurlemann et al. conclude that oxytocin "may selectively enhance learning where there is some prosocial component but aid forgetting where the overall learning context is experienced as highly aversive and stressful" (2010).

Now that we have shown oxytocin's bonding effect, let us discuss how these effects relate to the enjoyment of music. Daniel Levitin, a leader in the field of music and brain function, has shown that oxytocin is released into the brain when we listen to music that we like or when we sing or play instruments with other people (PBS, 2009). It is not a stretch, then, to expect levels of social bonding between those who listen or play music together on account of oxytocin. There are a variety of conclusions that we can draw from our knowledge of oxytocin and how it relates to both aforementioned sides of music performance: listening and playing. On the listening side, those who listen to music or watch a musical performance together often experience a greater feeling of closeness and intimacy after such experiences. Levitin claims that sharing musical experiences with another person increases this feeling of intimacy because of the release of oxytocin in the brains of both people while listening to music (PBS, 2009). When playing music together, whether it be in a drum circle or choir with even the simplest of songs, individuals experience a certain bonding that is unique to the musical experience. Playing music and singing together is fun! We can account for a certain portion of this enjoyability because of the observed oxytocin released in the brain. Oxytocin is additionally known to have a calming effect. One study showed that when playing calming music after intense and invasive medical procedures such as open heart surgery, the study saw that there was an increase in the release of oxytocin in the brain which provided a calming and comforting effect, allowing the patients the greater possibility for a steady recovery (U. Nilsson, 2009, p. 2160).

Next, let us examine the use and workings of the neurotransmitter dopamine in relation to musical enjoyment. "Dopamine is released by the nucleus accumbens and is involved in mood regulation and the coordination of movement" (Levitin, 2006, p. 121). It is not unique to humans, rather, it is also synthesized in many animals and plants. Because of this commonality that we share with other creatures, scientists can study the effects of dopamine on a variety of animals with ease. Dopamine is known for being part of the pleasure and reward system of the brain, but this is not the whole story. According to Chanda and Levitin, "there is an emerging consensus that learning and goal-directed actions are mediated by dopaminergic neurons in the VTA and their projections to the NAc and prefrontal cortex," or, in other words, "the emerging picture is that dopamine does not function as a 'pleasure' neurochemical per se, but rather, regulates motivation and goal-directed behaviors, playing a critical role in prediction and learning related to future rewarding events" (Chanda & Levitin, 2013, p. 180). So, dopamine, rather than being released as a 'pleasure' chemical in the brain purely for the sake of pleasure, is released in a regulatory and directional manner, in a purposeful manner. Dopamine changes our behaviour by changing our expectations within cause-and-effect circumstances.

Here we might see how dopamine can be related to music. Few studies have shown and observed the actual presence of dopamine in the brain during a music listening session, but it is not a stretch to make the connection. In 2011, Salimpoor et al. were the first to show that "the intense pleasure experienced when listening to music is associated with dopamine activity in the mesolimbic reward system, including both dorsal and ventral striatum" (Salimpoor, et al., 2011, p. 260). However, these results are not without caveats. The researchers continue to state that their results show that the musical choices "are perceived as being rewarding by the listener, rather than exerting a direct biological or chemical influence" and that the "results in a rewarding response are relatively specific to the listener, as there is large variability in musical preferences amongst individuals" (Salimpoor, et al., 2011, p. 261). This result is hardly surprising, because it is widely held that there are a great variety of musical tastes and likings, and to have one piece that the entire world finds pleasurable seems highly unlikely. Yet, the conclusion that Salimoor et al. present is not without use, and they themselves acknowledge this, as they state, "the notion that dopamine can be released in anticipation of an abstract reward (a series of tones) has important implications for understanding how music has become pleasurable" (Salimpoor et al., 2011 262).

As we mentioned above, dopamine relates to the pleasure and reward system in the brain by way of observing a cause and effect sequence. We might ask, where in a piece of music is the most exciting, rewarding, or enjoyable part? Now, of course, we might argue with one another and never come to a clear conclusion, but there are likely some themes or commonalities that we can point out. Usually, for a piece of music that follows a narrative structure, the most enjoyable part will be the climax. The piece would be structured in such a way that it leads our expectations toward a certain point, building anticipation and intensity, until its final release at the perfect moment. Other pieces might have a more consistent repetitive structure that continues to lead and entrance us by keeping with our expectations just enough to make it interesting. Studying the working of dopamine in the brain further exposes the correlation between expectations and foiled expectations, as well as pleasure and reward. Music is often an attempt to balance these aspects of life: to have just enough pleasure, just the right amount of delayed pleasure, and the perfect prolonging and fulfilling of our expectations.

The last neurotransmitter that we will discuss is serotonin. Serotonin is likely widely known because of its mood regulating properties. Indeed, many antidepressant pharmaceuticals like Prozac and Zoloft act as chemical mood modulators which send serotonin reuptake inhibitors in the brain which allow for the release of serotonin to last longer and create higher concentrations of serotonin in its synapses (Berger, et al., 2009, p. 6). Yet most of the serotonin in the body is produced and found outside of the brain, meaning that most of the serotonin used in the body functions outside of our cognitive capacities. This includes, "cardiovascular function, bowel motility, ejaculatory latency, and bladder control" (Berger, et al., 2009, p. 1). For our interests, however, we shall explore the effects that serotonin has on the brain and, again, how it relates to music.

When involved in the central nervous system, "serotonin is almost exclusively produced in neurons originating in the raphe nuclei located in the midline of the brainstem" (Berger, et al., 2009, p. 14). Serotonin, in one way or another, affects and regulates nearly all human behaviours. "The behavioral and neuropsychological processes modulated by serotonin include mood, perception, reward, anger, aggression, appetite, memory, sexuality, and attention, among others" (Berger, et al., 2009, p. 2). It is not surprising, then, that low serotonin levels likely correlate with low mood, depression, and poor memory. Conversely, ways to boost your serotonin levels include mood inductions like psychotherapy, increased exposure to natural light, exercise, maintaining a healthy diet, and of course, listening to music (McIntosh, 2018).

It would not be too bold of a claim to state that music has the ability to change our mood. If one of the main purposes of music is to express certain emotions or to have an emotional appeal, then an inevitable byproduct of that expression would be the affecting of mood. A sad piece of music, written and performed well, will make the listener feel sad. The same with an upbeat or happy song. Music can also affect our behaviour. Hardcore punk or metal music has been known to make people aggressive: jumping, pushing others, and breaking things. It can make us dance and clap, tap our toes and nod our heads. Of course, not everyone has this reaction to these genres of music, and it might not be simply the music itself that makes people react this way, but there is no doubt that music plays a key role. So, there are various responses that music has elicited that serotonin is also known to elicit. Is there a correlation? An increasing number of studies have shown that there is a possibility of correlation. A 2018 study, which examined how an auditory stimulus (music) affects rats, discovered that when listening to music, serotonin was released in the brain as well as dopamine (Moraes, et al., 2018, p. 77). This study was also noteworthy because it further indicates the relationship between serotonin and dopamine, showing that "serotonergic pathways may modulate [dopamine] activity in the [caudate-putamen (the dorsal striatum)] in response to music exposure" (Moraes, et al., 2018, p. 73). In other words, when music is played, serotonin interacts with dopamine in a unique way.

Our brief section on the relationship between music and chemistry has explored the ways in which our brain chemistry is influenced by auditory stimuli, specifically musical stimuli. We have looked at three different, but not unrelated, neurotransmitters, discussing first what their purposes are, then examining how they present themselves in our brain when we hear music. Oxytocin, likely the most researched and most known about of the three, brings people together and incites a special bond between two individuals. When we play or listen to music together we often create a stronger and more intimate relationship with one another, and oxytocin is partly responsible for this. We learned that dopamine is more than merely pleasure for its own sake, but is rather based on certain goals, expectations, and anticipated outcomes. Pleasure derived from music is often at its peak when our expectations are perfectly met, which often means that there are moments when our expectations are foiled. Finally, serotonin is the versatile neurotransmitter that has a wide range of uses, and is far more present in many regions outside of the brain than in the brain itself. However, within the brain, we saw that serotonin regulates our behaviours. We saw that it might not be simply a coincidence that music also influences our behaviours.

To sum up, exploring the world of neurochemistry allowed us to account for a significant amount of evidence as to why human beings like music. Although music does not seem to quell our basic evolutionary needs, it has lasted and lived among us for generations. We can explain why this is, at least from a scientific perspective, by showing that music elicits a clearly pleasurable response from the brain, evidenced by the presence of those neurochemicals known for their pleasurability. However, there is much more to research and explore in this domain, and scientists have only begun to understand how music affects our brain.

CHAPTER 3:
THE BIOLOGY OF
SOUND AND MUSIC

Both the physics of music and the chemistry of music are important in understanding the human relationship with music, but without biology we do not have a full understanding of that relationship. It is biology that connects the physics of music to the chemistry of music. It is not arbitrary that the specific vibrations produced by certain soundwaves cause our brain to release neurotransmitters. Biology is the path through which certain combinations of tones, pitches, and vibrations become oxytocin, dopamine, and serotonin - it gives us a complete understanding of the connection between music and sound.

Physics helps us differentiate between music and sound by explaining the nuances of pitch, tone, and vibration. By understanding these, we better understand music. Chemistry helps us differentiate between music and sound by explaining the triggers and impacts of neurotransmitters. But other parts of the body produce neurotransmitters, and the field of biology can bridge the gap between specific soundwaves and pleasure. How does it do this? Well, "the hearing systems in the ancestral lineage that led to [homosapiens] have evolved in response to stable environmental conditions as far as the physics of sound is concerned" (Reybrouck, Podlipniak, & Welch, 2019, p. 10).

Therefore, soundwaves existed before humans, and so it follows that the structures that humans developed to interpret soundwaves developed in a way to take advantage of soundwaves. Just like cities developed to take advantage of geological formations such as rivers and mountains, ears developed to take advantage of physics. And because physics follows reliable, stable rules, our evolutionary biological journey can be investigated. First, we will begin with the hardware: our ears - the aforementioned structures which humans developed to take advantage of physics. And then we will examine the software: our evolutionary programming which causes our brain to release neurotransmitters when certain soundwaves (i.e. music) are captured by our ears.

THE STRUCTURE OF THE EAR

The outer ear has three main features: the auricle, the ear canal, and the ear drum. The auricle is the part of the ear most of us are familiar with, as it is the only part of the ear we normally see - the outer flap. The purpose of the auricle is simple and easily understood: it "reflects sound towards the ear canal" (Brownwell, 1997, p. 3). Almost every person implicitly understands its purpose because at some point they have cupped their hands around their ears and therefore increased the surface area, which reflects more soundwaves toward the ear canal. Soundwaves travel down the ear canal and hit the eardrums - scientifically called the tympanic membrane - which turn the sound waves into vibrations (John Hopkins, n.d.). These vibrations continue their journey via the middle ear.

Not only is the middle ear between the outer ear and inner ear physically, it is between them in complexity. It is composed of several small, intricately connected bones that "conduct sound from the eardrum to the fluids of the inner ear" (Brownell, 1997, p. 3). They do this by acting as "mechanical levers [which] further increase the pressure of the sound at the entrance to the cochlea" (Brownell, 1997, p. 3). These small, intricately connected bones are known as the ossicles: the malleus, incus, and stapes, Latin for hammer, anvil, and stirrup, respectively (John Hopkins, n.d.). And, in a twist of evolutionary fate, the "tiny bones in the middle ear appear to have evolved from gills that were no longer needed" (Brownell, 1997, p. 3).The vibrations from the sound waves pass through the malleus, into the incus, and then into the stapes (the smallest bone in the human body), which is connected to the inner ear through the oval window (John Hopkins, n.d.).Although the outer ear is well-designed and the ossicles of the middle ear are certainly intricate, the inner ear is far more complex than either. It "contains the sensory systems of balance and hearing" (Brownell, 1997, p. 3), but for our purposes we will focus solely on hearing.

"The auditory portion of the inner ear of mammals differs structurally from that of birds, reptiles and fish but its function in all animals is the same - to tell the brain how much energy is contained in an environmental sound and at what frequencies that energy is located" (Brownell, 1997, p. 4). This is done via the cochlea - the smallest organ in the human body (Brownell, 1997, p. 1). The cochlea, "which is a spiraling structure" whose name comes from the "Greek word for snail" (Brownell, 1997, p. 6), is filled with fluid and nerve endings. The soundwaves were reflected by the auricle, down the ear canal, turned into vibrations by the ear drum, and passed through the ossicles. Now, they reach the fluid, which moves, setting the nerve endings into motion, which "transform the vibrations into electrical impulses that then travel along the eighth cranial nerve (auditory nerve) to the brain" (John Hopkins, n.d.). Our understanding of sound comes from the way our brains interpret these impulses. (John Hopkins, n.d.). These interpretations can lead to neurotransmitters being released, but why?

MUSIC AND HUMAN EVOLUTION

A simple way of understanding the relationship between the chemistry of music and the biology of music is thinking of the evolutionary biology as the context for the chemistry. Neurotransmitters such as dopamine reward us for certain actions, and it is easy to understand that by repeating those actions, we get rewarded. Because these neurotransmitters feel good, we seek out behaviours, conditions, and materials that produce them. And since we evolved to pass along our genes, it follows that we will be rewarded for creating behaviours, conditions, and materials that facilitate this goal.

Music does this through enabling communication. In fact, "music is a fundamental part of our evolution; we probably sang before we spoke in syntactically guided sentences" (Schulkin & Raglan, 2014, p. 1). Not only did it serve as an early form of communication, it also helped us continue to develop the increasingly complex forms of "communicative scaffolding for social interactions that have become so crucial or our species" (Schulkin & Raglan, 2014, p. 5).

Therefore, not only did music serve as a form of early communication, it continued to develop along with the society it helped create, which embedded it as a form of emotional system. As defined by Schulkin and Raglan, "emotional systems are forms of adaptation allowing us to, for instance, note danger through the immediate detection of facial expressions" (2014, p. 1). Just as we can communicate emotions through smiles and frowns, we can do so through music, which "cuts across diverse cognitive capabilities and resources, including numeracy, language, and spatial perception" (Schulkin & Raglan, 2014, p. 2). Solely through music, we can reasonably guess the emotions of people from a society completely different from our own, just as we can through facial expressions. As far as survival goes, this is important: reading body cues can tip us off to dangerous situations. Communicating emotions through music can help us create a happy situation.

But music, like the societies with which it is intertwined, is complex. Although we can often guess the emotions of foreign societies and cultures through music, without the aid of language or other emotional systems, this is not always true. Perhaps the solemn drumbeat of your culture that marks a death is the celebratory drumbeat of another culture that marks a wedding. And the emotional power of music can often fool people who do understand that same culture's language. For example, songs such as "Hey Ya" by OutKast mask sad lyrics with music most consider to be happy - and many listen to the song without realizing it is not a happy one, if lyrics are the emotional arbiter.

This complexity does not reduce the evolutionary importance of music, but enhances it by promoting prosocial behaviour: by understanding the music, you understand the society, and vice versa. The music's communicative abilities are "relative to a framework of understanding—a social context rich in practice, style and history" (Schulkin & Raglan, 2014, p. 4). By integrating yourself into the society, you integrate yourself into that framework of understanding, and therefore the society - which increases the chances of passing along your genes.

Biology is not more important than physics or chemistry when it comes to music. Each is an equally important building block in our understanding of the relationship between humans and music. But keep the lessons of biology in mind as you continue forward into the book. The importance of biology in human development is key to our next chapter, which discusses the psychology of sound and music: how the music we internalize through our body's biology affects us on a psychological level. The importance of music as an early form of communication and an emotional system will be further developed, especially in the third section of this book, where we will analyze two musical case studies to see exactly how music is intended to make us feel. The relationship between music and culture will also be further examined in depth in the final section of this book, which relates to politics and the political implications of music.

CHAPTER 4:
THE PSYCHOLOGY OF
SOUND AND MUSIC

There are a great many ways to connect psychology, sound, and music, and exploring some of the available connections will allow us to greater understand the ways in which we connect with music within our bodies. According to the Encyclopaedia Britannica, psychology is "a scientific discipline that studies mental states and processes and behaviour in humans and other animals" (2020). When we consider music from a psychological lens, then, we are considering the ways in which it affects us internally; how our mind categorizes, remembers, and reacts to it. Our study will take us through music and emotion, where we will consider how music can cause emotional mimicry, and music and the brain, where we will look at the connections between music, memory, therapy, and identity. By considering music from this lens, we will be better able to understand the emotional and memory aspects of music, which will help us as we continue our journey through this interdisciplinary study of music.

MUSIC AND EMOTION

Music is full of emotion, and has been since its very inception. At its core, music is communication: music speaks to us and tells us a story, both with and without words. When composers write music, they have an emotion in mind that they want to portray, whether it's pride, guilt, or sadness. Their goal is to make their listeners feel that emotion when they listen to their composition. The Encyclopaedia Britannica defines emotion as "a complex experience of consciousness, bodily sensation, and behaviour that reflects the personal significance of a thing, an event, or a state of affairs" (2020). In that sense, emotion is more than just the way we feel: it is the way we react to the way we feel based on our personal circumstance.

One of the most fascinating things about music is that it allows us to partake in emotional mimicry. Before we explain what emotional mimicry is, let's think for a moment. Think about a time where you were inconsolable. Would that get worse if you listened to a sad song, or a happy song? Could you have pulled yourself together if you had listened to enough empowering and happy music? Or, think about a time where you were really struggling. What sort of music did you listen to? Music that helped you continue to feel down, or music that empowered you to get back up and get back at it? When you are feeling happy, do you listen to music that encourages you to continue to feel happy, or do you listen to sad music to bring your mood down? There are many definitions for emotional mimicry based on the many ways in which it can be studied, but for the purposes of our study, emotional mimicry is exactly what it sounds like: mimicking emotions experienced around us. Here, we won't be talking about the emotions of people that are physically around us; instead, we will be talking about the emotions that are portrayed to us through the music we listen to, whether it's vocal or orchestral music.

While we will go into more detail about how music communicates emotion in the third section of this book when we discuss communications and the theory of musical semiotics, it is important to note that there are many different ways in which music communicates emotion to us. From a quick beat that makes us feel happy and uplifted to a slow beat that makes us feel relaxed, tired, or even sad, the music we listen to will always have an impact on the way we feel. For this reason, we can both consciously and unconsciously mimic the emotions of the music we listen to, thereby either bringing our mood up or down. A research study by Lisa Chan, Steven Livingstone, and Frank Russo looked at the ways in which viewers' facial expressions changed when they viewed videos of individuals singing different songs. They established that "happy singing performances elicited increased activity in the zygomaticus major muscle region of observers, while sad performances evoked increased activity in the corrugator supercilii muscle region" (2013, p. 1). In essence, when the people on-screen were singing happy songs, viewers used their smiling muscles, and when people on-screen were singing sad songs, viewers used their frowning muscles. That's just one way that music and emotion coincide.

It isn't just when people are together and can see each other singing songs that songs are capable of changing a person's mood: moods can change simply from listening to happy or sad music. One of the major ways in which this occurs is through the music's tempo. For example:

> Physiological functioning tends to mimic the musical expression, i.e., the rhythmic patterns, and through afferent physiological feedback, it elicits the emotion conveyed by the tempo (Scherer and Zentner, 2001; Dibben, 2004). Then, specifically for music, the positive (happy) and negative (sad) emotions effects in arousal might depend on musical elements composing the excerpt and not only to the quality of the emotion (Ribeiro et al., 2019).

This means that when tempos are high, music tends to be happier, and the body tends to exhibit a response with higher energy than music with a low tempo. To put this information into practice, let's think about the workout playlists we may or may not have on our phones. Most workout playlists consist of high-energy music with high tempos, energetic lyrics, and a general high-energy mood to them; very few workout playlists aside from stretching playlists consist of slow, low-energy, mellow music. The reason for this is quite simple: we feel better and more energetic when listening to happy music than we do when we're listening to sad music, and in moments when we need to pull all the energy in our bodies to focus on a physical task, we listen to music that will help us get in the right zone.

The ways in which music influences our emotions also depends on the social situations we find ourselves in while we are listening to music; after all, listening to music alone in a bedroom versus with a crowd of people at a concert are two very different experiences. According to research by Patrik Juslin and Petri Laukka, "the strongest emotional experiences often occur while listening alone (while listening attentively to the music), but it may also occur in social and emotionally charged situations" (2010, p. 232). Interestingly, depending on the person attending the concert and their connection to the artist and their music, the experiences of listening to music alone in a bedroom and at a concert could be a similar emotional experience, regardless of the physical differences. This goes to reiterate the fact that no two musical experiences are going to be psychologically the same for any two people.

There are hundreds of studies that have been completed on music and emotion from a psychological stance, and it would take many years and multiple books to lay all that information out. For the purposes of this book, we need to understand that music influences each person differently but that, in general, upbeat music tends to make people feel more happy, and mellow or sad music tends to make people feel relaxed or more sad. Determining happy versus sad music is usually done through analyzing the music's tempo (how fast the beat is) and general speed (the quicker, the more energetic). That said, based on their personal experience, knowledge of specific artists and their songs, and associations with specific songs, individuals will have different reactions to specific songs as regards the way the music makes them feel.

MUSIC AND THE BRAIN

Though we did spend the chemistry chapter discussing some of the particular chemical impulses which help our brain and body make sense of the way music makes us feel and helps us act on those feelings, it is important to also consider music and the brain from a psychological sense, as it is an additional perspective to help us understand the ways in which different music impacts us on a daily basis. This section will allow us the opportunity to explore some psychological studies conducted on the connections between music and memory, music and music therapy, and music and identity. This analysis will complete the book's science section, and leave us with a well-rounded understanding of some of the scientific ways to consider music.

Music, Memory, and the Brain

If I asked you to think about a specific song right now, what song would you think of? What associations do you have with this song? Why did you think of that specific song as you read through this section of your book? Our brain is capable of associating specific memories, thoughts, or ideas with the songs we listen to; in essence, creating a musical memory book somewhere inside our brains. Perhaps you were thinking about a specific song because you know you have a strong memory associated with it. Perhaps you thought of a song because it is the one you are currently listening to. Regardless of the reason, we associate memories with songs. How does this happen? As Tiffany Jenkins explains:

> The hippocampus and the frontal cortex are two large areas in the brain associated with memory and they take in a great deal of information every minute. Retrieving it is not always easy. It doesn't simply come when you ask it to. Music helps because it provides a rhythm and rhyme and sometimes alliteration which helps to unlock that information with cues. It is the structure of the song that helps us to remember it, as well as the melody and the images the words provoke (2014).

We have so much information stored in our brains that it's a miracle that our brain can sort through it all well and quickly enough for us to function. From the motions of breathing, walking, and moving our fingers to type, to recognizing and storing away social cues, words, and thoughts, our brains do an excessive amount of functioning just to keep us alive each and every day. Outside of that, we learn new things and we have to find new spaces to keep that information stored. And it's there, in the storage of information, that the correlation between music and memory becomes so interesting. The rest of this section will be dedicated to discussing some of the extensive research that covers music and memory, and considering how the results affect us and our everyday lives.

We will start off with the consideration of the neuroscience of how music and memory relate, through examining Christopher Bergland's claim that "listening to music engages large-scale neural networks across the entire brain" (2013). In 2013, a study by doctors Amee Baird and Severine Samson studied the way in which music affected memory recollection in individuals with brain injuries; in essence, trying to establish whether music would help people with brain injuries remember specific events in their lives. Excitingly, their findings "suggest that music is an effective stimulus for eliciting autobiographical memories and may be beneficial in the rehabilitation of autobiographical amnesia, but only in patients without a fundamental deficit in autobiographical recall memory and intact pitch perception" (Baird & Samson, cited in Taylor & Francis, 2013). This study was the first of its kind, and proved without question that music engages so many parts of the brain that injuries to specific parts of the brain means that memories associated with music in injured parts of the brain may be retrievable. As we will discuss later in this chapter, this study also supported music therapy, which is a way of helping individuals with brain injuries overcome parts of their injury through the help of music.

According to a group of researchers at Dartmouth College, "the brain's auditory cortex, the part that handles information from your ears, holds on to musical memories" (Dartmouth College, 2005). This means that when we have memories that are specifically associated with songs, they are stored in the auditory cortex. That doesn't mean, however, that all of our memories related to music are stored in the auditory cortex, nor does it mean that the auditory cortex is the only part of the brain associated with music and memory. Interestingly, in the same study:

> The researchers also found that lyrics impact the different auditory brain regions that are recruited when musical memories are reconstructed. If the music went quiet during an instrumental song, like during the theme from the Pink Panther, individuals activated many different parts of the auditory cortex, going farther back in the processing stream, to fill in the blanks. When remembering songs with words, however, people simply relied on the more advanced parts of the auditory processing stream (Dartmouth College, 2005).

In short, this study definitively proves that when we are listening to music, there are many aspects of our brain that are utilized at any given time: to anticipate the coming melodies, to store memories related to that specific song, or even to decode parts of the song's intent and emotional meaning. When the same researchers played a song while the participant was in an MRI and paused the song, they found that "people couldn't help continuing the song in their heads, and when they did this, the auditory cortex remained active even though the music had stopped" (Dartmouth College, 2005). Thanks to this research, we know that even when we aren't actively listening to music, our auditory cortex can still be functioning in the same way as if we are listening to music if, say, we are thinking about a specific song.

Another interesting study proved which exact parts of the brain decode and comprehend which aspects of the musical experience. This study analyzed such musical aspects as rhythm, tone, and timbre (tone colour), and then studied which aspects of the brain were utilized in decoding each musical aspect. They found that:

> The processing of musical pulse recruits motor areas in the brain, supporting the idea that music and movement are closely intertwined. Limbic areas of the brain, known to be associated with emotions, were found to be involved in rhythm and tonality processing. Processing of timbre was associated with activations in the so-called default mode network, which is assumed to be associated with mind-wandering and creativity (Akatemia, 2011).

By establishing which sections of the brain dealt with which musical aspects, these scientists allowed us to explore the way in which we process music in a more scientific and reliable way. Because of this, psychologists are better able to study the psychological effects of music on memory, emotion, and a variety of other aspects of the human body. For the purposes of this book, by understanding some of the many advances in research regarding music and the brain, we are able to successfully and comfortably delve into the next section, in which we will discuss different music therapy techniques and how effective they are in varying populations.

Music Therapy

Music therapy spans an entire clinical study, which is outside the scope of what this book intends, so when we discuss music therapy in this sense, know that we are discussing it in such a way as using music to help individuals with mental or physical illnesses find an aspect of peace through music. Whether it's listening to a song to feel comfortable in a moment of stress or to remember a specific time in one's life, music has been proven to be extremely therapeutic; it is in this sense which we use the term music therapy. With this in mind, let us consider some of the ways in which music can be therapeutic to those in most need.

With the knowledge that exists in the scientific world about the many ways in which the brain comprehends music, it seems natural that this knowledge should be exploited to assist those whose brain may serve them less efficiently. As one can imagine, studies regarding music and the elderly have been extensive and encompassing, as finding ways to help elderly individuals maintain a sharp mind is extremely important. For example, a 2014 study by Sara Bottoroli and her colleagues studied "the impact of different types of background music on cognitive tasks tapping declarative memory and processing speed in older adults," and established that "overall, background music tended to improve performance over no music and white noise, but not always in the same manner" (Bottoroli et al., 2014). Interestingly, this research seems to prove that even the simple act of listening to music engages the brain enough to provide assistance to other cognitive tasks occurring while the music is playing.

With results such as these in mind, it only makes sense to move forward to consider the ways in which music might be able to assist individuals with brain diseases such as Alzheimer's disease. Shirlene Moreira, Francis Justi, and Marcos Moreira did an extensive review of existing literature on the effectiveness of such treatments, and established that existing studies "showed the benefits of using music to treat memory deficit in patients with [Alzheimer's disease] (2018, p. 133). In fact, there are even some psychologists who believe that music may be the answer to finding a way to better understand Alzheimer's disease simply because of the ways in which music affects the brain: "as a neurobiological phememon [music] is multidimensional: these dimensions range from the decoding of abstract sensory signals potentially lasting several hours, to physiological responses that shift from moment to moment with sometimes surprising results (chills, tears, the tapping of feet)" (Clark & Warren, 2015). Regardless, the interest in music as regards aiding those with degenerative brain diseases remains.

Of course, the interest remains for good reason. Consider this, if an elderly individual with trouble recalling certain events in her life can listen to a song and recall every aspect of a certain previously-forgotten life event down to the fabric of her dress and the colour of the bows in her hair, what could that mean for her? Perhaps it means she can continue to use the oral tradition of storytelling to pass down stories to the next generation. Perhaps it means that she will feel less stressed, knowing that her memories are all locked up inside of her, but that music is the key to unlocking it. Perhaps it simply means that she can enjoy a moment's reprieve from her struggle to remember as she listens to a song and the memories come flooding back to her. Regardless of the method, the results are important: individuals who are older and struggle with memory for whatever reason are able to recall events based on a musical trigger.

Interestingly, music therapy isn't just used for the elderly: it has a multitude of uses for a wide variety of mental illnesses as well. For example, individuals with depression or anxiety can work to utilize music as a positive trigger, so if they feel high levels of anxiety coming on or are experiencing a major depressive episode, they are able to listen to a specific song and help themselves to feel comfortable and safe through positive association (J. Henschel, personal communication, July 31, 2020). That's not to say that said music can 'cure' the individual of a depressive state; instead, it suggests that a piece of safety, security, and happiness can be found for that individual within a specific song. Uses of music in this sense can be utilized for nearly everyone; after all, music has proven to elicit specific emotions from individuals, and when they know a song makes them feel a specific way, they can listen to it for the sole purpose of engaging with that specific emotion.

By considering the ways in which music can be used to jog a person's memory or provide them with a psychological safety blanket during a time of great need, we realize that music can be used to do a large amount of good in this world, which is likely one of the reasons that we continue to engage with new music each and every day. That said, the music we listen to has a huge impact on the individuals we shape ourselves into, based on a number of psychological factors. The final section of our psychology chapter will consider some of the ways in which music plays into our cultural and individual identities.

MUSIC AND IDENTITY

Music plays a large part in cultural identities, alongside which is an evident psychological identity. For instance, let us consider the cultural identity of the 1960s, and the way in which music influenced the cultural identity and personal identity of individuals in their prime at that time. The 1960s are a particularly good example of cultural identity because of the cultural revolution that occurred during that decade, with "the end of legal segregation, the achievement of legal equality for women, increased tolerance for homosexuality, concern for the environment, and heightened respect for non-western cultures" (Kurtz, cited in Berkowitz, 2003, p. 29). So many important cultural milestones were achieved during the 1960s, (though, admittedly, there was still a lot farther to go in many respects) that the identity of the decade was seemingly cemented in these achievements.

So how, then, did music play into the cultural identity of the 1960s? Well, as often seen in decades prior, the music of the time reflected the way that people were feeling and thinking. As Mikal Gilmore notes, "in particular, folk music (which had been driven underground in the 1950s by conservative forces) was now enjoying a popular resurgence. Under the influence of Joan Baez and Peter, Paul and Mary, folk was turning more politically explicit, becoming increasingly identified with civil rights and pacifism, among other causes" (1990). Music was the outlet that was utilized to express the way that young people felt about the state of their world. Songs like Bob Dylan's The Times They Are a-Changin' and the Beatles' Blackbird specifically discussed issues that they felt strongly about: from the end of segregation to the tension between tradition and what was desired to be the new tradition. Rock & roll, and music that speaks directly to the times are recognized as an important part of the 1960s, as historians consider the ways in which music created a cultural identity for individuals to partake in for both the purpose of feeling like a part of a group, but also because they wanted their voices and opinions heard, and the music of the time was helping do so.

Interestingly, cultural identity through music can be both a benefit and a detriment; on one hand, music can band people together as one with their beliefs, but on the other hand, music can deviantize an entire group who appreciate a certain type of music. For example:

> In the 1920s it was argued that the rhythms and instrumentation of jazz stimulated the sexual energies of youth and contributed to the 'outrageous' style of dancing (e.g. the Charleston), the physical appearance of young women (with short skirts, short hair, and makeup), and behaviors like smoking and drinking (especially in females)" (Bereska, 2018, p. 119).

Within this single statement, it is easy to see the ways in which the older generation marked jazz music as deviant because of the ways in which it was perceived to change the identities of the people who listened to it. Is this an accurate way of perceiving jazz music? Not at all - it wasn't the music that 'made' people change; it was their own desires that were reflected in the music, which is why they were able to enjoy it so fully.

That said, jazz music was an extremely important part of 1920s culture, and as the times go on, 1920s and jazz music are inextricably entwined in history.

This brings us further into our discussion about music and identity, in that cultural music identity is one thing, but personal music identity is a complete other. For example, let's consider the music we as individuals listen to. Perhaps we listen to an extensive amount of jazz music. Maybe we're more into classical symphonies. Perhaps modern pop music is more of our jam. Hair metal, anyone? There are hundreds upon hundreds of musical genres for each of us to explore, and the genres we choose to explore become a part of our individual identity in a variety of ways. For example, consider individuals that listen to gangsta rap music, and the way in which they are perceived. As the Encyclopaedia Britannica explains:

> Gangsta rap [is] a form of hip-hop music that became the genre's dominant style in the 1990s, a reflection and product of the often violent lifestyle of American inner cities afflicted with poverty and the dangers of drug use and drug dealing. The romanticization of the outlaw at the centre of much of gangsta rap appealed to rebellious suburbanites as well as to those who had firsthand experience of the harsh realities of the ghetto (2020).

Does this mean that everyone who listens to gangsta rap artists such as Ice Cube, Dr. Dre, and Snoop Dogg also romanticize the idea of the outlaw and want to act violently and do drugs as a reflection of the music they listen to? Not at all! Yet in some cases, the individuals who listen to this music are referred to as gangsta and are assumed to share the same values as their music simply because people identify the music a person listens to as a part of their identity, often incorrectly mixing the values of the music with the values of the person.

That isn't to negate music's impact on identity, however, because the impact is there, true, and undeniable. Not to say that every person that listens to gangsta rap is going to do drugs and act violently; that's the same as saying that people who listen to music from the 1960s are all peace-loving hippies. As sociologist Tami Bereska notes: "one of the reasons why youth media is deviantized is because of its presumed effects on youth" (2018, p. 119). It's those last four words - presumed effects on youth

- that make the most important difference here: just because people assume a person's identity is hugely impacted by their music doesn't mean that every bit of music they listen to is going to impact them in large and life-changing ways.

At the same time, the music we listen to has proven to be impactful upon our identities. As Chukwuma and her colleagues explain: "Music constructs our sense of identity through the direct experiences it offers of the body, time, sociability, experiences which enable us to place ourselves in imaginable cultural narratives" (2017). The music we listen to speaks to us and can impact the ways in which we choose to live our lives, but that doesn't mean that the music we listen to is the only aspect making up our identities. As we think about music and identity, we have to remember that there are hundreds of other influences on our identities that we experience every day: music is just a piece of the large puzzle that makes up who we are.

CONCLUSION

Through the first section in this book, we have considered music through the lens of science, looking specifically at the physics, chemistry, biology, and psychology of music. By doing so, we have offered explanations from the simplest way to consider the physical creation and existence of music to the ways that it impacts the release of chemicals in our brain. By understanding the fundamental, physical, and scientific ways in which music affects us, we will be better able to comprehend some of the softer and more abstract ways to consider music. As we move on from science, we will be moving into linguistics, where we will tackle the age old adage that 'music is a universal language' and establish the truth behind music as a language, musical notation, and the language in music and its effect on music itself.

SECTION 2: LINGUISTICS

CHAPTER 5:
MUSIC AS A LANGUAGE

INTRODUCTION

There is a long-standing notion that music is a universal language. Indeed, the similarities between language and music have long been pondered at by the world's greatest minds: "over 2,000 years ago, Plato claimed that the power of certain musical modes to uplift the spirit stemmed from their resemblance to the sounds of noble speech" (Patel, 2007, p. 3-4). Also, when considering that language and music are both uniquely human domains, it is no coincidence that there have been heavy comparisons between the two. In his book, Music, Language, and the Brain, Aniruddh D. Patel discusses the relationship, similarities, and differences between language and music at length. While Patel's discussion enters a level of complexity that is unnecessary for our discussion here, the insights and explanations about the two aural modes he gives can help to provide us with a firm foundation from where we can build a comprehensive understanding of the interlacement of language and music.

Before launching into our discussion of these two modes, it is important to define and have a working concept of what each aural mode actually is. We will begin with language. Laurel J. Brinton and Leslie K. Arnovick define language as such:

> Human language is a system. In other words, it is highly structured and operates according to a set of principles. Every language is governed by rules for the formation of words and sentences; these rules constitute its grammar. In order for us to learn a language, the set of rules must be finite in number, but with these rules we can produce an infinite number of sentences and understand sentences which we have never heard before. Theoretically, we could also produce sentences of

infinite length, though there are practical limits imposed by memory and the physiology of speech. It is for these reasons that we say human language is infinite or creative (2017, p.3).

It is important to note that the comparison being discussed here is between language and music, not English and music. There are over 7000 languages spoken on this earth and, while many of them are similar and fall closely to one another on the linguistic tree, others vary so differently from one another that form, structure, and sound have almost no comparison. Thus, when comparing music and language, we must first identify the universalities that span all languages and then compare those universalities with music. Brinton and Arnovick (2017, p. 4) have compiled the following list that encapsulates the ubiquitous attributes of language:

- All human beings have language.
- All languages are creative and symbolic.
- All languages use finite sets of discrete sounds.
- All languages are governed by finite sets of rules (i.e. grammar).
- All languages have similar grammatical categories (noun, verb).
- All languages contain semantic universals ('male', 'female', 'animate',
- 'inanimate', 'human').
- All languages make grammatical distinctions, such as past time, plural number, and negation.
- All language may be used to perform various speech acts, such as asking questions, issuing demands, and making promises.
- There are no primitive languages, except perhaps contact languages (i.e. pidgins).
- All languages change over time.

These are the characteristics that span all languages and it is from here that we will look to see how language and music are alike and, ultimately, whether or not music is a type of language. While it is important to remember we are talking about language and its traits in general, for simplicity's sake, when discussing some of the finer points of the structure of language we will largely be using examples that are pulled from English as we make the assumption that those reading this book are familiar with English in particular, if not exclusively.

BASICS OF LANGUAGE

As every human is born with the predisposition to learn language and we learn how to speak miraculously fluently and quickly at a young age, it can be difficult to appreciate the complexity that goes into understanding and speaking a language. We are all masters of our primary languages and thus, unlike other subjects like history or physics, all the complications and components that build a language are often unnoticed by its native speakers. Here, we will attempt to shed some light on the building blocks that work together to provide us with our main form of communication.

Firstly, there is phonology. Phonology is, "the study of the sound system of a particular language, the distinctive speech sounds, the combination of sounds that are possible, and features such as intonation and stress" (Brinton and Arnovick, 2017, p.4). Phonology can be viewed as the most basic building block when it comes to the foundation of language. A phoneme is a distinct sound of a particular language such as /s/ or /f/. After phonology, there comes morphology. This is the "study of the form and formation of words in a particular language" (Brinton and Arnovick, p.4). Morphology breaks down how phonemes, or distinct sounds, are combined into meaningful units of sounds, called morphemes. Examples of these include words, prefixes, and suffixes. Our next building block is the study of syntax. Syntax is defined as: "the study of how words are arranged into higher units, such as phrases, clauses, and sentences" (Brinton & Arnovick, 2017, p. 4-5). These three fields of study, phonology, morphology, and syntax, are the most simplified breakdowns of an approach to studying language.

In addition to the aforementioned building blocks, it is also important to consider semantics. Semantics have to do with the meaning of words. For example, a simple word like 'cat' can have an intension and extension meaning, a denotative and a connotative meaning, as well as other semantic features that might be particularly attributed to that word. While the music enthusiast might wonder why the fine print attributes of language, such as these, are relevant, it is important to have a working understanding of the complexity of language along with its basic building blocks in order to have the comprehensive tools needed to compare this aurel mode to that of music.

While we have already discussed thoroughly what music is and what it consists of, for the sake of this chapter's focus, it may be interesting to consider Patel's contemplations of what music is:

> There are very few universals in music. Indeed, if 'music' is defined as 'sound organized in time, intended for, or perceived as, aesthetic experience' (Rodriguez, 1995, cited in Dowling, 2001, p. 470) and "universal" is defined as a feature that appears in every musical system, it is quite clear that there are no sonic universals in music, other than the trivial one that music must involve sound in some way. For example, it is quite possible to have a modern piece of electronic music with no variation in pitch and no salient rhythmic patterning, consisting of a succession of noises distinguished by subtle differences in timbre. As long as the composer and audience consider this music, then it is music (Patel, 2007, p. 11-12).

Earlier in this chapter, we highlighted that when comparing music and language it is important to ensure that the comparison be between all languages and music, and thus compiled a list of universalities. As Patel so adeptly points out for us here, though, music's universalities are severely limited if not outrightly nonexistent. The subjectivity of what can be considered music is, most definitely, a perk of creative license. When comparing these two aural modes and wondering if music is a language, though, the lack of parameters in music becomes problematic. We are left then without the choice of comparing universalties between music and language and must therefore instead discuss the similarities and differences between the two based on the general attributes of each.

SIMILARITIES BETWEEN MUSIC AND LANGUAGE

As we alluded to earlier, language and music have long been interwoven in the minds of those who ponder the aural processing of humans. This is no surprise as humans are the only species on earth who are capable of and engage in both language and music. Of course, you might wonder, what about animals? Certainly, there are animals who make melodious sounds, there are even those winged creatures that are referred to as songbirds. Is this not music? As we consider all the discussions we have had so far about music, as well as the discussions yet to come, it is important to understand that music is a creative and meaningful pursuit, characteristics that the sounds of the animal kingdom lack. For example, though many species have mating calls, these calls are not purposefully composed or thought of, rather they are instinctual. As well, mating calls are not fluid in their meanings or semantics; they have a single, unchanging purpose - to find and attract a mate. It is for these reasons that while they may sound pleasant, animal sounds are not considered music.

With the sure knowledge that music and language are both exclusively human domains, it is time to explore some of the many similarities between the two aural modes. While there are those that lean toward the disposition of music and language having little in common and their comparison not being worthy of time, Patel clearly outlines basic similarities between the two modes before devoting a chapter to each in his book. He asserts these undeniable similarities by saying that language and music:

> Share a number of basic processing mechanisms, and that the comparative study of music and language provides a powerful way to explore these mechanisms. These mechanisms include the ability to form learned sound categories, to extract statistical regularities from rhythmic and melodic sequences, to integrate incoming elements (such as words and musical tones) into syntactic structures, and to extract nuanced emotional meanings from acoustic signals" (2007, p. 12).

Taking some of Patels insights, along with the knowledge we have gained thus far in the book, will help us to engage more thoroughly in the relationship between language and music.

As mentioned above, language and music are uniquely human but, in addition to that, language and music are also two of the only traits that span any and every human culture, no matter how different they are. Earlier we looked at the biological and chemical interactions that occur with our experiences with music. These interactions can also advocate for the similarity between language and music. Patel summarizes this well: "research suggests that although musical and linguistic syntax have distinct and domain-specific syntactic representations, there is overlap in the neural resources that serve to activate and integrate these representations during syntactic processing" (2007, p. 297). Simply put, the way our brains process these two aural modes in an extremely similar manner. If our brain processes these aural modes so similarly, are they indeed simply different forms of the same thing? Is music a type of language? Let us look at the composition of the two modes to come closer to an answer.

After a thorough debriefing on the elements of what music consists of in earlier chapters, along with the brief summary of the building blocks of language in this chapter, it will be fairly straightforward to analyze the alignments between the two. Structurally, both are particulate systems, meaning that both are a combination of elements that alone bear little or no meaning but once combined, form to create something more comprehensive and purposeful. Individual words or notes do little to achieve their purpose. But once combined in new and particular ways, the elements take on a whole new level of significance. It is also important to note that the elements of each are arbitrary, but gain purpose when combined together. Patel illustrates this similarity well:

> In language, there are syntactic principles that guide how basic lexical subunits (morphemes) are combined to form words, how words are combined to form phrases, and how phrases are combined to form sentences. In music, there are syntactic principles that govern how tones combine to form chords, how chords combine to form chord progressions, and how the resulting keys or tonal areas are regulated in terms of structured movement from one to another. In both domains, this multilayered organization allows the mind to accomplish a remarkable feat: A linear sequence of elements is perceived in terms of hierarchical relations that convey organized patterns of meaning" (2007, p. 264).

As we have witnessed, considering how we process music and language in a similar manner, it follows that each oral mode should have a similar hierarchical organizational structure.

DIFFERENCES BETWEEN MUSIC AND LANGUAGE

Despite these similarities, and many others that we didn't discuss here, it is also important to recognize and assess the other side of the spectrum: what are the differences between music and language? One of the most prominent differences is the way that music emphasizes pitch and rhythm in a way that language doesn't. While, of course, languages often fall into a certain pattern of metre when talking, with music, the pitch and rhythm is specific and purposeful. Another stark contrast between the two is that languages are heightened specificity when it comes to semantics. Music cannot communicate as clearly and specifically as language does although, of course, it absolutely does communicate, as we will discuss in the next chapter. Patel highlights these differences when saying:

> Language grammar is built from categories that are absent in music (such as nouns and verbs), whereas music appears to have much deeper power over our emotions than does ordinary speech. Furthermore, there is a long history in neuropsychology of documenting cases in which brain damage or brain abnormality impairs one domain but spares the other" (2007, p.4).

Patel draws our attention to how, even though language is a more effective form of communication, music is a more powerful resource when instilling emotions within someone or, to a greater degree, stirring up empathy. As well, despite how we discussed earlier that, cognitively, we process the two aurel modes similarly, research has also shown that the two can in fact function independently from one another within our brains.

Another important observation by Patel, and quite worthy of our notice, is the matter of translation. Translation serves as a particular problem for any person wanting to assert that music is undoubtedly a language. For instance, many books, poems, memoirs, diaries, or any other forms of literature have been translated time and time again. Best selling novels are often translated into multitudes of languages for audiences around the world to enjoy. Why is this so? Because, of course, the comprehension of a particular language must be learned. The relationship between the sound of a word and its connotative and denotative meaning are completely arbitrary and, thus, must be relearned for each individual language. Music does not suffer from this limitation. Though different cultures and places may enjoy particular types of music more, foreignness of sound can be quickly overcome with an open mind when it comes to music. Furthermore, while it is necessary in many instances to translate between languages, the concept of translation music into a spoken language, such as English, is quite strange. The process and objective of such an undertaking would be severely questioned. While of course there is the age old saying of there being something lost in translation, to translate music into language or vice versa would be a disservice to both.

CONCLUSION

While music certainly can speak to us, that is, move us emotionally, affect our mood, suggest or influence certain thought patterns or create cognitive associations, music is definitively not a language. One of the main reasons in support of this conclusion is music's lack of semantic meaning. If we refer back to our definition of language, we will recall that language can produce an infinite set of sentences and, furthermore those fluent in the language will be able to easily comprehend the precise semantic meaning of a sentence even if they have never heard it before. Where language differs from music then, in this example, is that a brand new sentence still has the exact same meaning for different people. The nuances of each combination of words convey the exact same concept, idea or notion to different people because there is a unwavering relationship between the words spoken and the definitions behind each of those words. Music, however, does not consist of this precision in semantics. This is neither a strength or weakness of either music or language when comparing the two; it is simply a considerable difference between the two aural modes. Additionally, while language can vary in its particular meanings slightly through things such as negative or positive connotations, Music has the much more fluid ability to 'speak' to individuals on a more personal level as each individual will listen to and interpret music in their own way, even if it is the exact same song. Overall, the interdisciplinary study of music and language is fascinating and is a conversation worthy of pursuit; however, despite their many shared characteristics, the two aural modes should be respected as distinct and separate forms.

CHAPTER 6: MUSICAL NOTATION

As we saw in the last chapter, music and language have many similar attributes. One further similarity that we will discuss at some length here is humanity's need to record their communications, be they linguistically or musically. For many centuries, music existed only in oral or instrumental form. Like language, the process of recording and/ or documenting sounds made simply did not exist. As time wore on, though, ancient societies began to feel the necessity of having some written form of their music. It is also not surprising that, as Gabriella F. Scelta describes, "systems of signs and symbols for writing music developed alongside written language as the need to pass along consistent information presented itself" (n.d., p. 1). So, just as writing began to form within societies, so did musical notation.

As we launch into our discussion of musical notation, it is important that we define it first: "a visual record of heard or imagined musical sound, or a set of visual instructions for performance of music. It usually takes written or printed form and is a conscious, comparatively laborious process" (Encyclopaedia Britannica, 2020). The earliest forms of musical notation can be traced back to multiple societies, suggesting that there was a ubiquitous need felt to 'pen down' the music of each culture. Ancient Egyptians, Summarians, and the Chinese all give evidence of having some form of musical notation in place. However, details of this ancient notation are hard to come by and there is, overall, little known about exactly what the notations of these various cultures looked like or how they functioned. For example, the ancient Summarians and Egyptians are known to assuredly have had hand signals that were "used to indicate the pitch, tone and shape of... melody" (Scelta, n.d., p. 1). This knowledge, combined with the evidence of their extensive hieroglyphics, suggests that these cultures did indeed have some form of musical notation. Additionally, as early as the third century BCE, the Chinese are known more definitively to have had a "sophisticated system of notation" (Scelta, n.d., p. 1). Now, 'sophisticated' here is a relative term. Compared to today, this system would seem archaic as it consisted of either symbols to represent vocalle syllables or symbols for an instrument. Lastly, in reference to ancient cultures, it is also known that the use of letters, particularly those of the roman alphabet, within musical notation was an adopted practice from the Greeks (Scelta, n.d., p. 1).

Following this timeline, there was relatively little advancement made in musical notation (that is known) again until the middle ages. This is no surprise: as Christianity began to gain power and control throughout Europe as a religion, musical notation, like almost every other aspect of society, was affected. In roughly 800 CE, the Roman Emperor Charlemagne, sought to unify and standardize all Christian religious practices, as they were widely varied from region to region. Music was a dominant aspect of the Christian faith and, thus, the myriad forms of musical notation that existed within the empire were wrought into one standardized form. This form, known as neumes, was limited in its ability to document music when compared to today, but was complex when compared to other, older methods: "any of various symbols representing from one to four notes, used in the musical notation of the Middle Ages but now employed solely in the notation of Gregorian chant in the liturgical books of the Roman Catholic Church" (Dictionary.com, 2020). Neumes have the ability to indicate the typical shape of a song. Thus, while they provided a firm foundation for today's musical notation to grow out of, they had their limitations. They were more often used as a reminder and a guidance of what was to be sung to someone who was already familiar with the song. Unlike today's musical notations, one could not look at neumes and learn a completely new piece.

Despite Charlamagne's efforts to unify musical notation, there was, of course, still a considerable degree of variance within it. In 1025, a significant improvement in music notation came at the hand(s) of an Italian monk named Guido of Arezzo (J. Bennett, 2015). He wanted to be able to enhance the speed and accuracy of his chanters so he devised a system for learning and remembering music more efficiently. By extracting vocalizations from the hymn Ut queant laxis, he created solmization or solfege; that is, using sounds designated for each note of the scale. The reader might know this system from the famous tune from

The Sound of Music called "Do Re Mi," singing, "Doe, a deer, a female deer," etc. Originally, Guido designated each note with the vocalizations, "ut, re, mi, fa, sol, la," with the "ti" not a part of the scale quite yet, and "ut" instead of "do". Next, Guido invented another helpful tool to be able to better follow and read neumes on a page: the staff. He put four lines on the page where neumes on which neumes could be placed to better indicate higher and lower pitches, and longer or shorter note values. He also, at the beginning of the staff, placed a marking that indicates the key of the piece, which we now know to be the clef, but in his case was usually a C or an F (J. Bennett, 2015).

After Guido's groundbreaking innovations, there was still a great deal to be improved upon. For one, it was still difficult to know how long the given note is supposed to be held, and, hence, rhythmic values were imprecise. This was improved upon by implementing a way to divide long stretches of neumes into smaller, equally measured groups, with the introduction of measure lines. With measures also came better demarcations for note values by creating four different types of rhythmic values: maxima (longest), longa (long), breve (shorter), semibreve (shortest) (J. Bennett, 2015). For reference, a breve is worth, in today's system, a double half note, and a semibreve is worth a whole note. After these four note values were introduced it was not too much longer before even smaller values were included: a minim (worth today's half note), a semiminim (quarter note), and a fusa (eighth note) (J. Bennett, 2015).

But measure markings cannot explicate much without a code to show precisely how much each note is worth. This is why time signatures were implicated. At first there were four time signatures that were called either tempus perfectum or tempus imperfectum. The former was divided into either three minims per semibreve and three semibreves per breve (equates to 9/8 time), or two minims per semibreve and three semibreves per breve (¾ time), and the latter was divided into three minims per semibreve and two semibreves per breve (6/8 time), or two minims per semibreve and two semibreves per breve (2/4 time) (J. Bennett, 2015). These four measure configurations were indicated by, in order, a circle with a dot in the middle, a circle, a half circle with a dot, and a half circle.

Eventually, much like the spelling of words around this time, the variances were subdued even further with the development of widespread printing practices. Just as the printing press created more consistency of language, so did it too with musical notation in the fifteenth century. With instrumental music on the rise in the seventh century, notation that was restricted to secular (instrumental) music was coming to the fore in church music, and therefore into the mainstream. Clefs, bar lines, notes, and measures all slowly evolved. Eventually, with a desire for more specified dynamics and articulations, those types of markings became more prominent. With the demand for more nuanced markings came the supply, with a touch of creativity.

These efforts are still being made today and, as music continues to evolve, so will musical notation. John Cage, Karlheinz Stockhausen, Pierre Boulez, and Luciano Berio are just a few examples of those who pushed the boundaries of musical notation (Scelta, pp.7-8). As always, with changes in styles and techniques, especially with movements such as the avant-garde, innovations in percussion music, or even styles like jazz and rock, necessitate new and more inventive markings on the page.

One extreme example of the development of musical notation are graphic representations of music. This type was born with the development of electronic music and is thus a good showcase of how musical notation reflects musical development. There are a variety of ways to denote musical sounds using graphic notation, and often the music denoted is intended to, at least in part, be improvised. Graphic notation systems include time-based pictographic scores which combine drawings and word descriptions of the desired sound with the specified instrument, and altered notation, which shows a usual score but in the altered shapes or staves with different contours. More abstract graphic scores can range from simply a picture or drawing, to what appears and scribbles all over the page. The possibilities for graphic scores are limitless, especially with improvements in computer technology in the last thirty years; scores are able to appear on computer screens and can therefore extend the creativity and possibilities for notation.

Thus, while Western notation is by far the most dominant form and is used in other parts of the world as well, there are still many varied forms of notations in existence and still many efforts to perfect said forms. As the music we make changes, so will music and as music changes so will its notation.

CHAPTER 7: LANGUAGE WITHIN MUSIC

After our thorough discussion on the similarities and differences between music and language, it will be interesting to discuss how one might potentially affect the other. To cover all possible effects would be nigh on impossible, thus, we will settle for some of the more salient ways that language can affect music. Before continuing on with this discussion, though, we should emphasize that this discourse will revolve heavily around the concept of perception. We can agree that both music and language are forms of communication and, like any type of communication, what is being communicated is subject to the recipient's perception. In other words, people will always have their individual interpretations of the communications they are on the receiving end of. With this subjectivity in mind, we will now take a closer look at how the language or lyrics within a song can affect the way we interpret music.

To help us with this interpretation, we will look to Pierre Schaeffer and his insights on the ways in which music and language simultaneously interact and conform to one another. He first borrows the outline of how language is orchestrated into meaningful expressions from Roman Jakobson:

> "'Speaking,' according to Jakobson, 'involves selecting certain linguistic units and combining them into more complex linguistic units. This is immediately evident at the lexical level: the speaker chooses words and combines them into sentences in accordance with the syntactical system of the language system he is using; these sentences, in turn, are combined into utterances. But the speaker is by no means an entirely free agent in the choice of words: the selection (with the exception

of very rare cases of true neologisms) must be made from the lexical resources he and the recipient of the message have in common.'" (Schaeffer, 2017, p. 234)

Here, it might be helpful to recall our summary on the building blocks of language - phonology, morphology and syntax - and understand that Jacobson is essentially illustrating how all of these blocks come together to form language. Schaeffer goes on, in addition to Jacobson's explanation, to relate how when constructing a sentence we are given only two options, selection and combination. We must select a meaningful unit and then combine it with other selections to form a coherent conveyance. Additionally, during the process of selection, we have the option of either substitution or juxtaposition (2017). What does all this mean? Well, to simplify, think about how you might go about choosing the words you are going to say to communicate something important to your significant other or the precise way you might write down a memory in your journal to capture its essence. Each word you choose has meaning, and the meaning of each word has a relationship to the other words it is joined with. These relationships of and between words actively influence our diction.

Now, what does all of this have to do with music? If we take Jakobson's above quote and "recycle" it, as Shaeffer has, the result is this:

> Making music involves selecting certain musical units and combining them into units of a higher degree of com-plexity. This is immediately apparent on the instrumental level. The musician chooses his notes [from them] and combines them into phrases in accordance with the system of counterpoint and harmony of the [musical] language system he is using; the phrases in turn are combined into 'pieces of music.' But the musician is by no means a completely free agent in the choice of notes: the selection [with the rare exception of completely new instruments] must be made from the musical code he and the recipient of the message have in common (2017, p.236).

Notice that the wording is the exact same except the language elements have been swapped out with musical ones. What does this mean? Although we concluded earlier on in this section that music is not a language, this is yet another example of their undeniable similarity. Essentially, the basics of language composition can be applied and substituted for the basics of music composition.

Now, any writer or composer will tell you that the art of arrangement is much more complicated than just selection and combination. Indeed, this seems to be an oversimplification. However, the fact that such a description aligns with both music and language so well invites questioning. Shaeffer's above analysis highlights for us that the context of words, or the specific word selection and combination, influences our perception on what is being said. The musical substitution of this same highlighted portion, then, indicates that the same holds true for music and that the context of notes, or the specific note selection and combination, influences our perception of what is being musically produced.

With these two conclusions in mind, it is not too far a leap to suppose that, with such similar structures, the context of words might affect the context of music. For example, say a particular song is being played, without lyrics, and the tone is generally agreed upon to be melancholic or sad. Then, let's say we add lyrics to this same song, the music itself has not been changed, but the lyrics are reminiscent of a fond memory. How might this affect how the song is interpreted? Now, perhaps, instead of the song be sad it might be more apt to describe it as bittersweet or nostalgic. These very particular emotions can be difficult to synthesize within someone if they are not authentically feeling it from a personal experience, or actually 'living through it' so to speak. However, music's ability to stir up emotion combined with language's semantic abilities are far more effective in producing a particular feeling, such as nostalgia, within someone versus either aural mode attempting the same feat alone. Thus, we can see how the overlay of music with words, be they lyrics, poetry or prose, might alter our perception of and have an effect on the music. We can see a culmination of the language and music together and that neither, individually, would have achieved.

In this example, we explored a way that lyrics and music might work together and take effect where each mode is complementary to each other. Referring back to Shaeffer's discussion, this was an example where the selection process consisted of substitution. That is, the feeling of sadness was substituted with one of nostalgia. The substitution, though, is one where both elements are on a similar spectrum. Sadness and nostalgia could be said to be closely related to each other emotionally. In other words, the music and language were not juxtaposed with one another, but rather brought about a similar, more particular substitute emotion.

What, if, though, the music and language of a song are juxtaposed?

Just as a filmmaker might overlay a happy scene with sad music or vice versa to produce a particular effect within the audience, a musician might choose to overlay sad lyrics with happy music. An example of this is Foster the People's "Pumped up Kicks." The song has an upbeat, lively tempo with a catchy chorus and fast pace. The lyrics themselves are not particularly well enunciated and, thus, it is not surprising that what the song is truly about actually eludes many people, even those that sing along to it. This elusion is only amplified by the music's deceptively cheerful sound. For context, Lyricfind.com (2020) provides us with the following:

> Robert's got a quick hand
> He'll look around the room, he won't tell you his plan
> He's got a rolled cigarette
> Hanging out his mouth he's a cowboy kid
> Yeah found a six shooter gun
> In his dad's closet, oh in a box of fun things
> I don't even know what
> But he's coming for you, yeah he's coming for you
> All the other kids with the pumped up kicks
> You'd better run, better run, outrun my gun
> All the other kids with the pumped up kicks
> You'd better run, better run, faster than my bullet

Evidently, the song is about a young kid who is about to partake in a school shooting. The topic is a sobering one and relevant to a crisis the United States has been struggling with for years now. Nevertheless, the song isn't as associated with the grimness that its topic usually is. We can never know for sure why exactly the artists chose to compose the song in this way, but it does not hurt to speculate. Certainly, once the catchy tune finally reveals its true topic to the listener, whether by repeated listings or a google of the lyrics, it is a shocking moment of realization. Perhaps, in this way, the song actually draws more attention to the crisis it sings about by catching the listener unawares. Regardless, just as words can be juxtaposed with words and notes can be juxtaposed with notes, music and language can be juxtaposed with each other to produce a certain perceived effect.

CONCLUSION

The relationship between language is vast, intertwined and, sometimes, unclear. Much has been devoted to the study of this relationship, and much still remains to be explored. While we have concluded that music is not a language in and of itself, it would be folly to argue against the clear and overt similarities they share. The written forms of both formed and changed in much the same ways along similar timelines just as each mode shares an almost identical compositional structure. As we leave this section involving the interlacement of these two aural modes it will be helpful to be mindful of what we have discussed in this section while we advance into a discussion on music and communications.

SECTION 3: COMMUNICATIONS

There are thousands of ways that music communicates to us: lyrics, instrumentation, and melody being only a few key examples. To break down each and every method of communication that music utilizes would be the result of a life's work dedicated to this sole topic. Instead, this section related to the ways in which music communicates with its listeners will be based on the theory of musical semiotics, which will provide us with the opportunity to develop an in-depth exploration of the ways in which composers ensure we understand music the way they intended us to. This section will take us through an introduction to musical semiotic theory, provide some examples of common ways that composers create connection and communication through specific choices in their music, and finally consider three case studies: one of Schubert's famous Lieder, the final movement in Berlioz's Symphonie Fantastique, and The Beatles' "Paperback Writer".

CHAPTER 8:
MUSIC VS FORM

In order to begin our discussion on musical semiotics, however, we must be able to distinguish the difference between music and musical form, since musical form is one of the predominant methods of communication in music. For the purposes of this chapter, we will consider music to be: "a pattern of sounds made by musical instruments, voices, or computers, or a combination of these, intended to give pleasure to people listening to it" (Cambridge Dictionary, 2020). This is the very same definition introduced in the book's introduction; the definition that will guide us through the coming chapter. Musical form, however, we will define as: "the structure of a musical composition" (Encyclopaedia Britannica, 2020). In essence, the difference between music and musical form is that musical form is the basis upon which music lives. Make important note of this distinction, as it will play into the coming discussion at many points.

THE EXPECTATIONS OF MUSICAL FORM

Let's say you decided to spend an evening at the symphony, to hear Beethoven's Fifth Symphony. Imagine your surprise, when you are greeted by the opening notes of a piano concerto instead of the symphony. Would you be disappointed? Curious? Perhaps a better example would be this: if you were listening to someone play the introductory notes to Beethoven's Fifth Symphony, you would expect the traditional 4 notes: dah, dah, dah, duh. What if only the first three notes were played? Your brain, knowing that fourth note should come, would be confused: why isn't the note there? That sense of expectation is known as musical expectation: the idea that once you have a certain amount of musical knowledge, you are able to subconsciously anticipate what should be coming next. As another example, singing a scale like "do, re, mi, fa, so, la, ti" would seem uncomfortable, because that final note - do - didn't appear at the end of the scale. You would expect the note to be there, and would feel uncomfortable until the note was added to the scale.

As Pearce & Wiggins, who studied auditory musical expectations, note:

> The ability to anticipate the future is a fundamental property of the human brain. Expectations play a role in a multitude of cognitive processes from sensory perception, through learning and memory, to motor responses and emotion generation. Accurate expectations allow organisms to respond to environmental events faster and more appropriately and to identify incomplete or ambiguous perceptual input (2012, p. 625 - 626).

As humans, our anticipatory tendencies help us survive each and every day, whether it's anticipating the killer jumping out from behind the door in a movie or anticipating the sound of thunder after seeing a lightning strike. In some ways, our anticipatory reflexes help keep us alive: we anticipate that crossing the street while there is fast traffic is dangerous, we anticipate the car in front of us slowing down when they turn their brake lights on, and we anticipate a painful landing if we jump from a swing that's too high off the ground. Interestingly, these anticipations tend to make us more comfortable, in that we might not jump when we see the killer jump out from behind the door, and we will hopefully wait until it is safe to cross the street instead of walking out in front of a car. Our musical expectations also help keep us safe in a way: by using our musical expectations, we are helping ourselves understand what will come next in the music; making us feel like we are in a comfortable environment where we know what comes next.

Musical expectation also translates into musical form. As we discussed in the introduction, there are basic aspects to many musical forms that are generally followed as rules; for example, there are typically 4 movements to a symphony based on the following outline: quick sonata form, slow sonata form, minuet form, and a fast sonata or rondo form. If a symphony was to start with a minuet, it would be unexpected, simply because musical expectation states that a symphony begin with a quick sonata form. Much like you would be surprised if your favourite rap music began with a harpsichord solo, you would inevitably be surprised by a symphony having a first movement that isn't in sonata form.

That being said, research has proven that not everyone will have the same level of musical expectation. Through their experiments, Loui & Wessel (2007) established that "musically trained individuals were sensitive to harmonic expectation, whereas musically untrained individuals were unaffected by different harmonies (p. 1090). The ability to distinguish expectations for a harmony is far more complicated than the expectation of a 'do' at the end of a scale, yet it is important to note that only the people with musical training were able to express their harmonic expectations: demonstrating the importance between the people with an excellent sense of their musical expectations, and the people who are more inadvertent with their musical expectations.

When our musical expectations are not met, when the fourth introductory note of Beethoven's fifth symphony is not played for example, we experience a feeling called cognitive dissonance. Cognitive dissonance can be described as "the distressing mental state caused by inconsistency between a person's two beliefs or a belief and an action" (Griffin et al., 2015, p. 200). For example, let's consider a person who smokes, but also enjoys running for physical activity. Stopping to smoke at the end of a run would cause cognitive dissonance, because this person believes that they are running for their health, but then smokes which they know is bad for their health. Until this inconsistency is resolved, they will feel uncomfortable: this discomfort is a sign of cognitive dissonance.

In the same way, cognitive dissonance is what you experience when you hear the first three notes of Beethoven's fifth symphony without the fourth. You know the fourth note should be there, and the composition feels incomplete until you hear that final note, which completes the sequence and makes you feel comfortable again. Now, it's important to remember that not everybody who listens to music is going to feel the same way about it; in fact, some people who listen to a symphony wouldn't even notice if the first movement was in minuet form. On the other hand, when musical expectations aren't met, history shows that the results can be devastating.

Consider Igor Stravinsky's composition The Rite of Spring. Its debut performance happened in Paris on May 29th, 1913, and as reporter Amar Toor notes, "it began with a bassoon and ended with a brawl" (Toor, 2013).

The Rite of Spring was a type of experimental modernist ballet that had never been seen before: "a frenetic, jagged orchestral ballet that boldly rejected the ordered harmonies and comfort of traditional composition" (Toor, 2013). Because the audience was expecting something more traditional than Stravinsky provided them, they reacted against the cacophony of sounds and dances in front of them with nothing short of terror. Even the story behind the ballet itself was nothing short of terrifying, "for the scenario is a pagan ritual in which a sacrificial virgin dances herself to death" (Classic FM, 2020).

From the first notes of the bassoon to the introduction of dancers to the stage, the ballet drove the audience to madness. The crowds catcalled and hurled vegetables at the performers and orchestras. Fights broke out amongst audience members. Ballerinas struggled to hear the orchestra over the cries of the audience. For an orchestral performance, the debut of The Rite of Spring was a massive disaster; and yet, the show went on during the rioting and after obnoxious crowd members had been ejected. Now, over one hundred years later, it is well known for being one of the most turmoil-ridden orchestral debuts in history.

The Rite of Spring does, however, give us a perfect, albeit extreme, example of the importance of expectations when it comes to musical form. That's not to say that each composer should religiously keep to musical form to meet the expectations of their audiences, because that is not only foolish, but also doesn't leave room for the creative liberties that often make musical compositions so unique and enjoyable. It is to say, however, that such a wild jump to left field when all musical expectations are set firmly in the right field can cause emotions to boil over in the individuals whose expectations are not met. The debut of The Rite of Spring was a once-in-a-lifetime event, for certain, but it reminds us that there are individuals who will be extremely unsatisfied - who will feel an excessively uncomfortable form of cognitive dissonance - until their expectations are met.

MUSICAL SIGNPOSTING

Now that we've learned about the importance of musical expectations, and some of the wild events that can occur when these expectations aren't met, we wonder: how is it that composers find a balance between meeting expectations and exceeding expectations? Why is it, for example, that The Rite of Spring disgruntled a crowd into chaos, whereas few other orchestral pieces can claim the same fame? One of the reasons this could be is musical signposting.

Signposts are an important part of our everyday lives: they tell us where our shops are in the shopping mall, where to turn off the highway to get to our friend's house, and more recently, what COVID-19 restrictions are in place at a particular place at a particular time. In essence, they direct us to the places we are going, while also reminding us of where we are at a particular moment in time. Musical signposts work in a similar way: it's the composer's way of telling us where we are in a musical piece, and where we are on our way to. Most of these musical signposts are built into specific musical forms, but on occasion and particularly when composers are breaking away from pre-existing musical forms, they will utilize musical signposts to help ease the transition where they feel necessary. For example, think about the expectation that the authors set with this book. Throughout the introductory chapter, each new section begins with a short quote. As we move into the chapters, short quotes no longer begin sections or chapters. We create an expectation that there will be short quotes beginning each new section, and then break the expectation because the quotes are no longer necessary once we move into the meat and potatoes of the book. This is a prime example of signposting, and the selective use of signposting.

Let's consider the way most pop songs are organized: introduction, growing tension with a strong beat, short pre-chorus, chorus, return of the tension with a strong beat, short pre-chorus, chorus, bridge, chorus, conclusion. Interestingly, the Canadian band Marianas Trench wrote their song, Pop 101, which is an entire pop song instructing listeners on how pop songs are put together while also following the typical pop music structure. Regardless, this structure builds in signposts that tells listeners where they are in the song. For example, the short pre-chorus exists for the sole purpose of reminding listeners that the chorus is coming up next: a feature particularly helpful to the people who only know the words to the chorus. The bridge, similar to the bridge in the symphony, connects two parts of a song, letting listeners know that they are near the end of a song , but that there is still one chorus left before the end. The vast majority of pop songs are written with this signposting method in mind, again creating musical expectations.

Signposts don't just occur in pop music either: they are present in virtually every type of music in existence because of the need to either meet musical expectations, or to help create musical expectations. As we move into the next chapter, focused on the theory of musical semiotics, we will realize that signposts form a particularly important function in music, even though the ability to recognize them is often more intrinsic than extrinsic. Before we move on, however, we have to remind ourselves of the difference between music and form: that musical form creates the backbone upon which music is created, that expectations regarding musical form are created through repetition within the same type of music, and that musical signposting is one way to manage expectations for musical form.

CHAPTER 9:
THE THEORY OF
SEMIOTICS

A BRIEF INTRODUCTION TO SEMIOTICS

Before we jump specifically into musical semiotics specifically, let's take a moment and explore the theory of semiotics in itself. Doing so will provide us with the basis to understand the difference between semiotics and musical semiotics, and will also give us a semiotic platform upon which we can base our understanding of musical semiotics. Semiotics is "the study of the social production of meaning from sign systems; the analysis of anything that can stand for anything else" (Griffin et al., 2015, p. 327). Though the definition sounds widely encompassing, before we elect that the definition itself is simply too broad, let's take a moment to deconstruct the definition and see what we can discern from it.

Before we begin to deconstruct the definition, however, we need to make a few things clear; the first of which is our definition of a sign. For the purposes of this chapter, and all other discussions regarding semiotics in this book, a sign is "the inseparable combination of the signifier and the signified" (Griffin et al., 2015, p. 328). The signifier, then, is "the physical form of the sign as we perceive it through our senses; an image" and the signified is "the meaning we associate with the sign" (Griffin et al., 2015, p. 328). To be clear: when it comes to semiotics, a sign does not mean a physical wayfinding sign. By the aforementioned definition of a sign, a sign could be bellbottom jeans representing the height of fashion in the 1970s or the term BLM, which represents the black lives matter movement. In essence, a sign is a physical thing that we associate meaning with.

Now that we understand what a sign is, let's begin deconstructing the definition of semiotics. "The study of the social production of meaning from sign systems" holds a lot for us to deconstruct. First, let us consider the part of the definition we are least likely to recognize: sign systems. According to Roland Barthes's theory of semiotics, which Griffin and his colleagues discuss in their textbook A First Look at Communication Theory, there are two types of sign systems: denotative and connotative. Denotative sign systems include "descriptive signs without ideological content" (Griffin et al., 2015, p. 331), whereas connotative sign systems include "mythical signs that have lost their historical referent; form without substance" (Griffin et al., 2015, p. 332). A road sign, then, would be a denotative sign, since they have no ideological content: their sole purpose is to tell you exactly where to go. A connotative sign is defined by its historical reference, so something like an old oak tree on your childhood property would be considered a connotative sign, as it is defined as a connotative sign by a small group of people (your family) because it has meaning to you, but it would be a denotative sign to anyone else because that meaning isn't clear. In the same way, a road sign near a crash site that killed a loved one may be a connotative sign to certain people, whereas it would exist as a denotative sign for the majority of the population.

"The social production of meaning" brings another question to the mix: what constitutes social production of meaning? If we take a moment and think about it, everything in our lives revolves around the social production of meaning. Everything from the clothes we wear (what really dictates office-wear versus party-wear?), the music we listen to (what makes us gangster if we listen to rap music?), to the ways we act every day (why is sneezing without covering your mouth and nose unacceptable when there's someone right in front of you?) has been shaped by the way society perceives meaning. Wearing a tank top and booty shorts to a law office would likely be frowned upon because society recognizes that law offices are a part of higher society, wherein we are expected to represent ourselves with dignity and in more formal wear, which a tank top and booty shorts do not represent. Grandparents might suggest that their grandchildren are out of line for listening to rap music, because they may associate rap music with criminals and drugs, even though there is no reason for them to do so other than that they believe rap music to be deviant. Sneezing without covering your mouth and nose when there is someone right in front of you is not only unsanitary, but is also perceived by the majority of society as being disrespectful. When we consider these examples, we are able to begin to understand the way in which society produces the meaning of essentially all aspects of our lives.

Another example we can consider is this: what does it mean if I hold up my pointer and middle fingers to make a V, while holding my ring and pinky fingers to my palm with my thumb? In the majority of the world, this is known as the V sign, or more typically, the peace sign. The thing is, not everywhere in the world considers it a peace sign; in fact, it is an extremely offensive gesture in certain cultures. For example, if my palm faces me and the back of my hand faces the person I am signing to, the gesture refers to the number two in American Sign Language, but is also an extremely insulting gesture in the United Kingdom and Australia. If my palm faces the person I am signing to and the back of my hand faces me, I could be referring to victory, to peace, or to the letter V in American Sign Language. Here we have the case of a single sign that has different meanings based on individual signifiers and signifieds.

With these examples and definitions in mind, understanding the definition of semiotics becomes easier. Interestingly, when considering the world through a semiotic lens, it becomes infinitely more complicated, because every movement, action, word, and thought has a web of signifiers and signifieds behind it that make up the way the individuals around us interpret our actions, and vice versa. With this in mind, we can begin to realize the ways in which musical semiotics can have a wide impact on the ways in which we consider music from a communication theory lens, and ask the question: what is the music saying?

MUSICAL SEMIOTICS

Musical semiotics was introduced to the world in the 1960s and 1970s, and has grown exponentially in popularity, to the point where it exists in three branches of academic study: "either as a branch of general semiotics, as the application of some general semiotic theory to music, or as a subdiscipline of musicology" (Tarasti, 2018). Many theorists were a part of its inception, including Roland Barthes, Charles Sanders Pierce, and Eero Tarasti. In essence, the concept of musical semiotics followed that of semiotics fairly closely, arguing that there are specific signs and symbols in music that hold important meaning to various audiences. Now, there is a large spectrum of literature focusing on musical semiotics, and since this is not intended to be a literature review, what we need to understand is that the general field of musical semiotics is wide, vast, and well represented.

Our specific study of musical semiotics revolves around two individuals: Roland Barthes, who was a semiologist (a person who studied semiotics) and philosopher who lived from 1915 to 1980, and Charles Sanders Peirce, one of the fathers of semiotics who lived from 1839 to 1914. As Griffin and his colleagues note: "Barthes was interested in signs that are seemingly straightforward but that subtly communicate ideological or connotative meaning and perpetuate the dominant values of society. As such, they are deceptive" (Griffin et al., 2015, p. 327). While Barthes was a semiologist and only dabbled in musical semiology, his semiotic studies into mass communication will play into our later discussion in our case studies. Interestingly enough, Barthes and Peirce considered semiotics differently: whereas Barthes focused on the tangible in the form of mass communication, "Peirce included non-verbal signs in his semiotic theorizing right from the start. He classified signs by type based on their relationship to what they represent" (Griffin et al., 2015, p. 335). These classifications will become particularly important to us as we attempt to decipher the signs present in two musical case studies, and as we help you, our readers, learn how to determine where musical signs exist in the music you listen to on a daily basis.

According to Peirce, there are three different types of signs that exist in our everyday lives, signs that we need to understand to be able to analyze the upcoming case studies. The first type of sign is a symbolic sign, which "bear no resemblance to the objects to which they refer. The association is arbitrary and must be learned within the culture as a matter of convention" (Griffin et al., 2015, p. 336). For example, let's consider our language. For people who haven't learned the English language, words bear no resemblance to their meaning. Each of the words you are currently reading was, at some point, arbitrarily created and attributed a meaning, which you learned within your culture. In that way, written language, down to each individual letter, is a symbolic sign.

The second type of sign is an iconic sign, which "have a perceived resemblance with the objects they portray. They look, sound, taste, smell, or feel similar to their referents" (Griffin et al., 2015, p. 336). The most basic example of an iconic sign is a picture: the sign represents the person in the photograph, yet is not actually the person in the photograph. This type of sign can take a while to wrap your head around, but when we think about the existence of photographs and realize that a photo of a pipe isn't a pipe itself - it is a photo of a pipe - we understand completely how iconic signs are determined.

The last type of sign we will consider is an indexical sign, which "are directly connected with their referents spatially, temporally, or by cause and effect. Like an index finger, they point to the object, action, or idea to which they refer" (Griffin et al., 2015, p. 336). Indexical signs are one of the easiest types of signs to understand, because there is a sense of logic to their explanation. For example, smoke would be an iconic sign, because oftentimes smoke represents fire. In the same way, thunder represents lightning, a laugh represents happiness, and a compass represents direction.

Being able to recognize these types of signs in our everyday lives makes life just a little bit more fascinating, because as we discussed, signs make up every aspect of our existence. Not only that: our newfound understanding will help us have a deeper understanding of the inner workings of the world around us, but it will also help us unravel the mystery that is music. To do this, we need to take our newfound understanding of the history of western art music and the building blocks of some of the most common musical forms in western art music, and apply the theory of semiotics to them. By doing so, we will be able to establish the ways in which musical form, notes, keys, and instrumentation have an affect on the ways in which we understand, appreciate, and experience music.

Now, before we go on to do this, we need to address an important question: why is this important? Why should we be learning to deconstruct music so we can build it back up again? Why does it matter? Well, to be quite honest, understanding music and the way it communicates with you should be an essential building block for your life, not just because it is interesting, but because it impacts and influences everyday actions you take. Music is, quite literally, a part of every aspect of your life. It plays while you work. It plays while you relax. It plays while you work out. It plays while you watch television. It plays in the car on your way home from work. It plays before your birth and after your death in honour or memory of you. Music is always available to you, if it isn't already playing in the background.

That said, different types of music have different types of effects on people. For reasons many of us don't know, upbeat music makes us happy, and slow music makes us sad. Music marks memorable moments: perhaps hearing a certain song reminds you of happy memories like your first kiss or your wedding, or perhaps they make you sad as they remind you of the song playing in the background when you got news about a death in the family. Music is there for us every inch of our lives, and its impact on us is undeniable. That said, music isn't always impacting an individual; sometimes it impacts a group of individuals.

The obvious example here is a concert: each individual attends a concert for a specific reason, but they are all there because of their collective love for the artist playing. Each person is going to hear the song in biologically the same way, but it is going to have a different effect on each of them based on their history with the song. For some, it will make them feel ecstatic, for others, it will dredge up sadness and heartbreak. They are physically experiencing the song in the same way, but the way the song makes them feel is different.

That is not always the case, however. Consider this example: when you go shopping in a shopping mall, there is different music playing in each store, and even music playing in the halls between stores. This is no accident. There has been extensive research on the ways in which different types of music affect shopping habits, which means that different stores are playing different music to make you feel a specific way: a way that that store wants you to feel. For example, if you are shopping for bras, stores will play music with sexy themes to make you feel sexy so you want to take home one of their bras. If you are shopping in a sports store, the music will be more invigorating and high energy to encourage you to feel pumped up and ready to work out using their products. This is just one of the ways that music can indirectly and nigh imperceptibly influence the decisions you make on a daily basis: without you even noticing.

The study of semiotics is important by itself, but the study of musical semiotics is even more important, because it's the study of the ways in which music influences you. It sounds terrifying to think that we can be manipulated by music, but in some slight ways, we can be. For this reason, it's important to be able to decipher the ways in which such control might occur, and establish how we can realize when music is manipulating our emotions. It's essential to remember that, for the most part, music is focused on making you feel a specific way: that is one of its fundamental purposes. We also need to remember that the majority of the time when you hear music, it's not intended to make you act in a certain way, but that in certain cases, like in a shopping mall, it can be. As we move into the next section, we will be dissecting two fascinating pieces of music to discover some of the ways in which they achieve their purpose: to make us feel a very specific emotion through music.

CHAPTER 10: WHAT IS THE MUSIC SAYING?

The essential purpose of this chapter is to find an answer to one of the most key communication questions when it comes to music: what is the music communicating to us? Now, this isn't some future-esque time when we can talk about how music controls our minds and tells us exactly what to do and how to act: not at all. Instead, we can look at the ways in which music directly influences us as individuals, remembering that no two songs are going to have the exact same impact on an individual: the way we connect with each song is going to depend entirely on our own personal experiences and knowledge.

Before we jump into our case studies, which are going to be extremely helpful in practically establishing some of the ways in which songs can be analyzed using the theory of semiotics, there are a few concepts we should cover that will help preface the way in which we will be attacking our case studies. As with most things, like surgery, construction, and essay-writing, having a plan before starting is extremely important, so we will start with explaining our method of attack, and looking at some of the ways in which our plan will be of benefit to our analysis.

We will start our analysis by looking at the big picture: what form the composition takes, whether it has lyrics, who composed it, and who is performing it. This will lead into the intention of the composition: what did the composer want their audience to feel? From there, we can start to break the composition down even further, noting what instruments are used and in what ways, as well as establishing the basic theme for the composition and how it is provided to listeners. By establishing the composition's big picture, we'll have a better understanding of how some of the smaller details fit in.

After we look at the big picture, we'll consider some of the smaller picture details, such as word choices in lyrics that relate to the theme, particular musical themes or commonalities that relate to us in some way, and even some new or unexpected ways in which the composer tries to impart their theme and emotion upon their listeners. By looking at these small and occasionally seemingly insignificant aspects of the composition, we will be able to get inside the composer's head and see exactly how each of their choices was made to help improve the listener's experience.

The case studies we have selected were not random: there are important musical aspects to each of the case studies that will help us take a wide view of just a few of the hundreds of thousands of ways that composers engage their listeners. Schubert's Erlkönig is a famous Lied focused on a story of a man and his dying son. The Lied is well known, its story is well known, and it utilizes many specific musical techniques to match the words that the original poet wrote. Our second case study looks at the fifth movement of Berlioz's Symphonie Fantastique, which is a well known program symphony with a fascinating story that utilizes non-traditional musical methods to engage its audience. Finally, we will consider a modern song: The Beatles' "Paperback Writer". Our analysis would not be complete if we did not consider a song where the composer wrote both the lyrics and the music, as well as a song that relates to deep and internal emotions. After we complete our analysis, we will quickly discuss our findings, and look at some of the ways in which our semiotic analysis changed depending on the type of musical composition we were considering.

CASE STUDY I: SCHUBERT, ERLKÖNIG

Before it became a Lied, the Erlkönig was published as a poem by Johann Wolfgang van Goethe. Goethe was an extremely famous poet, playwright, and novelist, amongst his other interests, and the Erlkönig was one of his most recognized works. The poem tells the story of a father and his young child who are racing home on horseback. As the story continues, it becomes clear that the young child is sick, as he insists to his father that he sees the Erlkönig, and that the Erlkönig is offering to take him away. As the poem advances, the Erlkönig moves from beckoning and bribing to threatening force upon the child, but when the child tells his father, his father does not believe him. The poem ends on a sombre note, when the father finally arrives at the house only to find his child dead in his arms.

The Erlkönig himself is a legend from a traditional Danish ballad, and while there is still debate on the technical translation of Erlkönig, the general consensus is that he is a dark elf king (Lumen Learning, 2020). The Erlkönig poem has been used in many Lieder by various composers, but the most well-recognized composition is the version by Franz Schubert. Even in the composition by Schubert, there are a wide variety of piano-singer duos that have performed the song, and for that reason it is important to clarify that the version we will be discussing is the version with Julius Drake on piano and Ian Bostridge performing the vocals.

Below is the Erlkönig poem in German, as well as the English translation.

Erlkönig

Johann Wolfgang von Goethe

Wer reitet so spät durch Nacht und Wind?
Es ist der Vater mit seinem Kind:
Er hat den Knaben wohl in dem Arm,
Er fasst ihn sicher, er hält ihn warm.
„Mein Sohn, was birgst du so bang dein Gesicht?"
„Siehst, Vater, du den Erlkönig nicht?
Den Erlenkönig mit Kron' und Schweif?"
„Mein Sohn, es ist ein Nebelstreif."
„Du liebes Kind, komm, geh mit mir!
Gar schöne Spiele spiel' ich mit dir;
Manch' bunte Blumen sind an dem Strand,
Meine Mutter hat manch gülden Gewand."
„Mein Vater, mein Vater, und hörest du nicht,
Was Erlenkönig mir leise verspricht?"
„Sei ruhig, bleibe ruhig, mein Kind:
In dürren Blättern säuselt der Wind."
„Willst, feiner Knabe, du mit mir gehn?
Meine Töchter sollen dich warten schön;
Meine Töchter führen den nächtlichen Reih'n
Und wiegen und tanzen und singen dich ein."
„Mein Vater, mein Vater, und siehst du nicht dort
Erlkönigs Töchter am düstern Ort?"

The Erlking

English Translation by Richard Wigmore

Who rides so late through the night and wind?
It is the father with his child.
He has the boy in his arms;
he holds him safely, he keeps him warm.
'My son, why do you hide your face in fear?'
'Father, can you not see the Erlking?
The Erlking with his crown and tail?'
'My son, it is a streak of mist.'
'Sweet child, come with me.
I'll play wonderful games with you.
Many a pretty flower grows on the shore;
my mother has many a golden robe.'
'Father, father, do you not hear
what the Erlking softly promises me?'
'Calm, be calm, my child:
the wind is rustling in the withered leaves.'
'Won't you come with me, my fine lad?
My daughters shall wait upon you;
my daughters lead the nightly dance,
and will rock you, and dance, and sing you to sleep.'
'Father, father, can you not see
Erlking daughters there in the darkness?'

107

„Mein Sohn, mein Sohn, ich seh es genau:
Es scheinen die alten Weiden so grau."
„Ich liebe dich, mich reizt deine schöne Gestalt;
Und bist du nicht willig, so brauch ich Gewalt."
„Mein Vater, mein Vater, jetzt fasst er mich an!
Erlkönig hat mir ein Leids getan!"
Dem Vater grausets, er reitet geschwind,
Er hält in Armen das ächzende Kind,
Erreicht den Hof mit Mühe und Not:
In seinen Armen das Kind war tot

'My son, my son, I can see clearly:
it is the old grey willows gleaming.'
'I love you, your fair form allures me,
and if you don't come willingly, I'll use force.'
'Father, father, now he's seizing me!
The Erlking has hurt me!'
The father shudders, he rides swiftly,
he holds the moaning child in his arms;
with one last effort he reaches home;
the child lay dead in his arms.

Text provided courtesy of Oxford Lieder [www.oxfordlieder. co.uk]

Translation © Richard Wigmore, Author of Schubert: The Complete Song Texts, published by Schirmer Books, provided courtesy of Oxford Lieder [www.oxfordlieder. co.uk]

The Lied begins strongly, with an intense and strong piano motif that immediately provides tension to the song. As Kerman and Tomlinson note, "the opening piano introduction sets the mood of dark, tense excitement. The right hand hammers away at harsh repeated notes in triplets, representing the horse's hooves, while the left hand has an agitated motif" (2015, p. 235). By introducing this motif from the very beginning, tension is built immediately: with the speed and intensity of the piano, listeners immediately can tell (thanks to the symbolic sign connecting speed and intensity to tension) that this piece isn't a happy one. The aggressive piano rhythm is also extremely tricky to play, and is one of the reasons that the piece is so difficult and agonizing for pianists: they must build up a lot of endurance in their hands to continue such a quick and strong pace throughout the entire piece.

The lyrics then begin overtop the piano, bringing a new level of depth to the piece. The lyrics are split into four 'voices' (all sung by the same person): the narrator, the father, the child, and the Erlkönig. "Each voice characterizes the speaker in contrast to the others. The father is low, stiff, and gruff, the boy high and frantic. Marked ppp [pianissimo] and inaudible to the father, the ominously quiet and sweet little tunes crooned by the Erlkönig [...] add a chilling note" (Kerman & Tomlinson, 2015, p. 236). Without having multiple singers, Shubert ensured that listeners would be able to decipher each character from the other, and also give the listeners a chance to learn more about each individual character through the voice he provided them. These specific tones also offer the singer the opportunity to embellish specific words or phrases to give them more impact; for instance, when Ian Bostridge sings the line "so brauch ich Gewalt/I'll use force," he changes from the Erkling's light and quiet voice to a harsh voice full of venom and aggression, snapping the listener to attention and making them realize that the Erlkönig is deadly serious about his intentions.

An important note to make, that will be brought up again in more detail during the second case study, is the key in which the song is written, and whether the characters sing in the major or minor key. Now, key isn't something we have discussed at length, so before we talk about the key specifically within the Erlkönig, we will talk about the use of key in general. In its most basic form, a key is "the major or minor scale around which a piece of music revolves. A song in a major key is based on a major scale. A song in a minor key is based on a minor scale" (Pouska, 2020). In general, we can consider the major key to be the 'comfortable' key, and the minor key to be the 'uncomfortable' key. What we mean by that is songs that are played in the major key tend to be generally happier and make the listener feel more comfortable, and songs played in the minor key sound and feel more odd and off putting.

Now, there is a purpose for the major/minor key difference, outside of musical technicalities. As Richard Parncutt notes: "the minor triad has a more ambiguous (less salient) root than the major, and the minor scale has more variable form and a more ambiguous (less stable) tonic; uncertainty is associated with anger, sadness, distress, and grief" (2014). Because we have a tendency to prefer stability in the majority of our lives, including our music, we feel more comfortable listening to music that is played in a major key than we do in a minor key. Let's consider how this factors into the Erlkönig. First off, the song itself is written in the key of E minor, which is a key associated with the feelings of "grief, mournfulness, restlessness. Like a princess locked in a tower longing for her rescuer and future lover" (LedgerNote, 2020). When we consider the story of the Erlkönig, we realize that the key specifically speaks to the story itself, helping Schubert feed his audience the emotions he wants them to feel.

Not only that: each character sings in either a major or minor key, relative to the key of the song. The father's character is sung in a major key, reflecting his more calm and controlled manner, particularly when he's telling his son that everything is going to be fine and the Erlkönig doesn't exist. The son's character is sung in a minor key, reflecting his distress as the Erlkönig comes closer and closer to him, before finally taking him away. Even the narrator's character is in a minor key, which functions to help set the tone for the entire piece, particularly since it's the narrator's voice that starts and ends the Lied. In general, by having the song set in the key of E minor and having specific voices set in major and minor keys, Schubert is directly communicating to his audience exactly how he wants them to feel about each character, and the entire Lied as a whole. Another important note to make about the Erlkönig is the fact that it is through-composed: "a song with new music for each stanza of the poem; as opposed to strophic [songs with repeating lyrics]" (Korman & Tomlinson, 2015, p. 429). If we think about most modern pop songs, we remember that their structure includes a return to a set of lyrics; in through-composed works like the Erlkönig, there are no lyrics, for the song instead continues to tell the story without repetition. There are, of course, benefits and negatives for using both forms, but in the case of the Erlkönig, having a through-composed work makes most sense because it allowed Schubert to stay true to the original poem, written by Goethe, without changing it to accommodate lyrics. Interestingly enough, there were very few Lieder that have lyrics, simply because of their typical structure in following the poem they were written for.

There are hundreds more ways we can consider the ways in which various musical techniques were used to help Schubert's Erlkönig to such success, but some of the most important aspects have been covered above. The biggest takeaways from this case study should be the importance of a composition's key, and the way in which key and composition can come together to tell their own story before the lyrics even begin. With these takeaways in mind, let's move forward to our second case study, where we will consider a composition with no lyrics, but that still tells a wild and exciting story through innovative and interesting musical techniques.

CASE STUDY II: BERLIOZ, SYMPHONIE FANTASTIQUE, V MOVEMENT

The story behind Symphonie Fantastique is one chock full of the wild and weird, and the symphony itself is representative of Hector Berlioz's life in more than one way. As Kerman and Tomlinson aptly put, "no other great composer has survived so unpromising a beginning to reach so unhappy an end as Hector Berlioz" (2015, p. 251). Berlioz (1803 - 1869) was born to parents who wanted nothing more than for him to be a medical student, directly in opposition to his own wishes to be a musician. He eventually became a musician against their wishes, and even then found a lack of support for his work by the general public, for his program symphonies "had simply no precedent and were not matched in ambition until the time of Gustav Mahler, about 1900" (Kerman & Tomlinson, 2015, p. 251). He suffered two dysfunctional marriages, one of which was to Harriet Smithson, who played an extensive part in his Symphonie Fantastique. In the end, he died alone and in pain from the heartbreak of the death of many of his loved ones including his son.

Regardless of his difficult life, and the fact that he was not recognized for the musical genius he was until long after his death, his musical talent was many years ahead of the composers at the time. As we will soon learn, his Symphonie Fantastique broke many traditional symphonic rules, and it has been said that the symphony "broke upon the world like some unaccountable effort of spontaneous generation which had dispensed with the machinery of normal parentage" (Beecham, 1959, p. 183). Berlioz is now recognized as one of the fathers of the program symphony.

As we mentioned earlier, Symphonie Fantastique is a program symphony, which tells a distinct story throughout it, often through a pamphlet handed out at the beginning of the concert that tells the audience what they should be looking for. For Symphonie Fantastique, Berlioz wrote the story himself, and what a wild story it is. As PBS notes, "Through its movements, it tells the story of an artist's self-destructive passion for a beautiful woman. The symphony describes his obsession and dreams, tantrums and moments of tenderness, and visions of suicide and murder, ecstacy and despair" (PBS, 2020). Berlioz based the symphony on his own life and his love for actress Harriet Smithson. The story carries through five movements: Reveries-Passions, A Ball, Scene in the Fields, March to the Scaffold, and Dream of the Night of the Sabbath. An entire book could be dedicated on its own to the semiotic analysis of this work; for that reason and with that fact in mind, our focus will be solely on the final and most interesting of the movements: Dream of the Night of the Sabbath.

For easy reference, Berlioz's original program notes are below, thanks to the New York Philharmonic (2019):

Part One: Reveries, Passions — The author imagines that a young musician, afflicted with that moral disease that a well-known writer calls the vague des passions, sees for the first time a woman who embodies all the charms of the ideal being he has imagined in his dreams, and he falls desperately in love with her. Through an odd whim, whenever the beloved image appears before the mind's eye of the artist, it is linked with a musical thought whose character, passionate but at the same time noble and shy, he finds similar to the one he attributes to his beloved. This melodic image and the model it reflects pursue him incessantly like a double idée fixe. That is the reason for the constant appearance, in every movement of the symphony, of the melody that begins the first Allegro. The passage from this state of melancholy reverie, interrupted by a few fits of groundless joy, to one of frenzied passion, with its gestures of fury, of jealousy, its return of tenderness, its tears, its religious consolations.

Part Two: A Ball — The artist finds himself in the most varied situations — in the midst of the tumult of a party, in the peaceful contemplation of the beauties of nature; but everywhere, in town, in the country, the beloved image appears before him and disturbs his peace of mind.

Part Three: Scene in the Fields — Finding himself one evening in the country, he hears in the distance two shepherds piping a ranz des vaches in dialogue. This pastoral duet, the scenery, the quiet rustling of the trees gently brushed by the wind, the hopes he has recently found some reason to entertain — all concur in affording his heart an unaccustomed calm, and in giving a more cheerful color to his ideas. He reflects upon his isolation; he hopes that his loneliness will soon be over. — But what if she were deceiving him! — This mingling of hope and fear, form the subject of the Adagio. At the end, one of the shepherds again takes up the ranz des vaches; the other no longer replies.

Part Four: March to the Scaffold — Convinced that his love is unappreciated, the artist poisons himself with opium. The dose, too weak to kill him, plunges him into a sleep accompanied by the most horrible visions. He dreams that he has killed his beloved, that he is condemned and led to the scaffold, and that he is witnessing his own execution. The procession moves forward to the sounds of a march that is now somber and fierce, now brilliant and solemn, in which the muffled noise of heavy steps gives way without transition to the noisiest clamor. At the end of the march the first four measures of the idée fixe reappear.

Part Five: Dream of a Witches' Sabbath — He sees himself at the sabbath, in the midst of a frightful troop of ghosts, sorcerers, monsters of every kind, come together for his funeral. Strange noises, groans, bursts of laughter, distant cries which other cries seem to answer. The beloved melody appears again, but it has lost its character of nobility and shyness; it is no more than a dance tune, mean, trivial, and grotesque: it is she, coming to join the sabbath. — A roar of joy at her arrival. — She takes part in the devilish orgy. — Funeral knell, burlesque parody of the Dies Irae [a hymn sung in the funeral rites of the Catholic Church], sabbath round-dance. The sabbath round and the Dies Irae are combined.

We will remember that there were typically only four movements in a symphony, and adding a fifth movement was just one of the ways that Berlioz distinguished his work from that of traditional composers. This fifth movement is in fugue form, and is in E-flat major, a key which typically feels "cruel, hard, yet full of devotion" (Ledgernote, 2020) and denotes "conversations with God" (Ledgernote, 2020). The movement begins in an unclear key with an unstable melody until the idee fixe is introduced.

The idee fixe is a supremely important piece of Symphonie Fantastique, so it is important to introduce and understand it before moving forward. Kerman and Tomlinson explain that an idee fixe is "a fixed idea, an obsession; the term used by Berlioz for a recurring theme used in all the movements of one of his program symphonies" (2015, p. 425). In this case, the idee fixe represents his love, Harriet Smithson. This theme, or motif, transforms in various ways (instrumentation, key, speed, and style) based on the way the main character, Berlioz himself, is feeling about his love at a particular time during the symphony. In the case of the final movement, the idee fixe is played shrilly and in a mocking way on the clarinet, demonstrating the way in which Berlioz sees Harriet Smithson welcomed to the orgy to mock the death of himself, her lover.

The overall instrumentation in this movement is important to note semiotically, as there are a variety of ways in which instrumentation is used to create feelings of uncertainty and discomfort. One of those ways is through the general instrumentation: it is played by clarinets, low brass, strings, and an organ. In general, these instruments might not seem like they can create uncertainty and discomfort together, but when we analyze how they work together in this movement, we see the instruments acting as symbolic signs, directing listeners to feel a certain way. For example, the clarinets play together in a purposefully squeaky melody that makes listeners uncomfortable: they are used to hearing perfectly tuned clarinets. The low brass plays in minor keys, and in the background, creating an unsettling background effect. In fact, "mutes are used in the brass instruments - perhaps the first time mutes were ever used in a poetic way" (Kerman & Tomlinson, 2015, p. 252). The organ, which is a tremendously fascinating instrument with a history of use solely for funerals that is typically played in death-related settings, brings another symbolic sign to the table: one that makes listeners realize that they are listening to a death tune without actively knowing why. The association between the organ and death is unconscious, and so the sign often goes unnoticed except when actively pointed out. Finally, Berlioz uses a variety of innovative techniques with the strings, such as the col legno, which involves playing the string instruments with the wooden side of the bow, creates new and jarring sounds for the listener to decipher. Individually, the specific instrumentation may not appear to have a technical effect on the listener, but with all the innovations together, these effects have a large impact on the listener's experience.

Berlioz also uses funeral bells to bring about the end of the first dance, before moving into an extremely contentious use of a religious tune. About this decision, Kerman and Tomlinson say:

> Berlioz prepares his most sensational stroke of them all - a burlesque of one of the most solemn and famous of Gregorian chants, the Dies irae (Day of Wrath). This chant is the centerpiece of Masses for the Dead, or Requiem Masses; in Catholic France, any audience would have recognized the Dies irae instantly. Three segments of it are used: each is started first in low brasses, then faster in higher brasses, then, faster still and in the vulgar spirit of the transformed idee fixe, in woodwinds and plucked strings. It makes for a blasphemous, shocking picture of the witches' black mass" (2015, p. 253)

To a large crowd of religious folk, the Dies irae is a sacred chant, and to use it in such a burlesque manner can be seen as nothing more than blasphemy. The fact is, however, Berlioz's use of it was intended to be so; he wanted his listeners to feel enraged, insulted, and as uncomfortable as possible during the use of the Dies irae, because by doing so, he gave life to the witches and made listeners feel as if they truly were watching this ineffable display of horror and turmoil. By blaspheming something that many of his listeners held dear to them, he brought to the surface the most raw of their emotions, opening the floodgate to allow them to experience a symphonic movement as they never had before.

Not only that: at the end of the fifth movement, Berlioz does something that's almost more unimaginable than blaspheming the Dies irae - he combines the witches' dance, which he begins the movement with, with the Dies irae to "drive home the point that it is the witches, represented by the theme of their round dance, who are parodying the church melody" (Kerman & Tomlinson, 2015, p. 253). Through this combination, he is not only using the Dies irae in a non-traditional place, but also combining it with a harsh and uncomfortable witches dance to ensure that his listeners truly experience the final movement with disgust and discomfort in their hearts. The final movement of this symphony is filled with layer upon layer of discomfort - whether brought upon by instrumentation, musical choice, or innovative musical techniques - to communicate to the listener without a doubt the exact way they should be feeling.

The final musical symbol we will discuss regarding this composition is the use of dynamics. We have talked about dynamics briefly, but to recap, dynamics is "the volume of sound; the loudness or softness of a musical passage" (Kerman & Tomlinson, 2015, p. 424). The quietest dynamic in a piece is pianissimo, represented in musical notation as pp. This is for passages that are intended to be next-to-silent, so audiences have to strain to hear them. From there, the next dynamic is piano, p, which is soft and quiet. Next comes mezzo piano, mp, which is moderately soft, in contrast to the next dynamic, mezzo forte or mf, which is moderately loud. As we get into the louder dynamics, we find forte, f, which is loud, and fortissimo or ff, which is very loud. Dynamics can be considered symbolic signs, as they have no direct relation to what the music is portraying: the way we react to a change in dynamics is a learned cultural behaviour.

Berlioz uses dynamics in a fascinating way during the final movement of Symphonie Fantastique in that he uses crescendos (moving from soft to loud) and decrescendos (moving from loud to soft) both abruptly and gradually when it suits his purpose. Aggressive crescendos tend to jolt audiences, again making listeners feel a sense of discomfort as they are shocked to move from quiet to loud in such a short time. At the same time, aggressive decrescendos similarly shock listeners as they are suddenly required to strain their ears to continue to hear the music. Gradual crescendos are a method of signposting within music: it takes listeners from slow, quiet music to the loud, full, and exciting moments in the composition and, when it's time, returns them back to the slow, quiet moments. Through using this symbolic sign throughout his composition, Berlioz is guiding his audience to how they should feel: comfortable when he moves them slowly from one dynamic to another, and uncomfortable when he forces them from pianissimo to fortissimo extremely quickly. This is just another method of communication he uses to include his audience in the emotions of this composition.

As we stated near the beginning of this case study, a full analysis of this piece would take many chapters; perhaps an entire book in itself. Instead, we have covered some of the main ways in which Berlioz uses musical signs and symbols to connect with his audience and ensure they feel the emotions he intends. From his choice of instrumentation and each instrument's historical connotation to his use of the Dies irae in a disrespectful and blasphemous form to purposefully incite anger in his audience to his use of dynamics to shock and calm his listeners, it is safe to call Berlioz a master at using musical signs to enforce the emotions he wants his audience to feel as they listen to Symphonie Fantastique.

CASE STUDY III:
THE BEATLES, "PAPERBACK WRITER"

The Beatles are unquestionably one of the world's most popular and influential bands of the twentieth century. The four boys from Liverpool, Paul McCartney, John Lennon, George Harrison, and Ringo Starr jumped onto the music scene in the 1960s and enthusiastically began to fundamentally change and question the ways in which popular music existed around them. Their story is long and fascinating, and could easily fill many books, but for the purposes of this case study, it is necessary to know only a brief history of the band itself, as well as a musical history explaining some of the musical techniques they utilize.

On July 5, 1957, 15-year-old Paul McCartney met 16-year-old John Lennon, cementing one of the greatest musical partnerships of all time. From there, Paul's friend George Harrison joined the Quarrymen, as they were calling themselves at the time, and after they removed their original drummer, Pete Best, to accommodate Richard Starkey Junior (Ringo Starr), the Beatles were formed. Their first single Love Me Do, peaked at number seventeen on the charts in the UK, but when they released Please Please Me, their first LP record, in America, they shot straight to number one. February 9, 1964 was another day for the books because when the Beatles played on the Ed Sullivan Show, approximately 73 million Americans cried, screamed, and sang along to the moptop boy band from Liverpool (History.com, 2020). The band went on to release 13 studio albums, 13 EPs, and 22 singles before their breakup in 1970. They transitioned from a touring band to a studio band before they released the unexpected and fascinating Sgt Pepper's Lonely Hearts Club Band, and stayed a studio band until their breakup. After 1970, the four never played together again.

"Rooted in skiffle, beat, and 1950s rock and roll, the Beatles later experimented with several musical styles, ranging from pop ballads and Indian music to psychedelia and hard rock, often incorporating classical elements and unconventional recording techniques in innovative ways" (Jhain, 2020). From their original rock and roll style, they transitioned to include classical elements in songs like Yesterday, began to include psychedelic elements with songs like Lucy in the Sky with Diamonds and Tomorrow Never Knows, demonstrated the influence of Indian classical music on their sound through songs like Within You Without You, and confidently transcended many genres and musical styles to find their own sound, which was a unique and beautiful amalgamation of all of their individual and collective influences. At the beginning of the 1960s, their instrumentation consisted of percussion, voice, guitar, and bass, but by the end of the decade, there were no limits to their instrumentation: they utilized everything from full orchestras to sitars in their journey to create new and engaging music that reached their audience in ways they had never been achieved before.

The specific song we will be discussing, "Paperback Writer", was released as a single in June of 1966, with Rain on the B-side. Interestingly, the concept for the song came from a request by one of Paul's aunts, who wanted him to write a song that wasn't about love. "With that thought obviously still in his mind, [Paul] walked around the room and noticed that Ringo was reading a book. [Paul] took one look and announced that he would write a song about a book" (Turner, 2018, p. 151). This song marked a specific point in Beatles songwriting, wherein they were feeling "less motivated by commercial demands and more focused on musical development" (The Beatles Bible, 2020). It was at this time that the Beatles began their transition to a fully studio band, as opposed to a touring band.

It's also important for us to consider the way in which the song itself is formed, particularly since "Paperback Writer" finds itself in a unique category of songs that are formulated like other types of media. "Paperback Writer" is written in a letter format: a letter from a writer to a potential publisher. The lyrics, courtesy of AZ Lyrics (2020), are below:

Paperback writer

Dear Sir or Madam, will you read my book?
It took me years to write, will you take a look?
It's based on a novel by a man named Lear
And I need a job, so I want to be a paperback writer
Paperback writer

It's the dirty story of a dirty man
And his clinging wife doesn't understand
His son is working for the Daily Mail
It's a steady job but he wants to be a paperback writer
Paperback writer

Paperback writer

It's a thousand pages, give or take a few
I'll be writing more in a week or two
I can make it longer if you like the style
I can change it round and I want to be a paperback writer
Paperback writer

If you really like it you can have the rights
It could make a million for you overnight
If you must return it, you can send it here
But I need a break and I want to be a paperback writer
Paperback writer

Paperback writer

Paperback writer, paperback writer
Paperback writer, paperback writer
Paperback writer, paperback writer
Paperback writer, paperback writer (fade out)

Though the letter itself goes unsigned, but from the very beginning of "dear sir or madam will you read my book" we are introduced to the epistolary format, something which is reasonably uncommon in songs in general, and something that was a first for the Beatles themselves. The letter format functions as an iconic sign, because the song represents the theoretical letter that the writer was writing to his potential publisher. The letter format also encourages listeners to delve into the story of the song - to recognize the character singing the song as opposed to thinking that Paul McCartney, who sings the main vocals, really wants to get his paperback book published. The Beatles' utilizing the letter format for "Paperback Writer" just adds another symbolic element to their song, which in turn provides another layer for listeners to peel back as they begin to understand the semiotic meaning within the song.

Now, before we begin a semiotic analysis of the song itself, we need to understand the context of the song by learning a bit about paperback books. To begin, we must remember that paperback books are substantially cheaper than hardcover books, both to produce and to purchase. After WWII, there was what the Encyclopaedia Britannica calls the "paperback revolution," which saw "paperbacks beg[in] to proliferate into well-printed inexpensive books on every conceivable subject, including a wide range of first-class literature" (2020). Previously, books had been borrowed instead of bought simply because of their extensive cost, regardless of paperback or hardcover. At this time, many books were being reissued in paperback, including books that had "been out of print for years, and that had been issued originally in small editions of no more than 2,000 copies by university presses or other specialized publishers" (Encyclopaedia Britannica, 2020). In essence, by publishing in paperback, books were becoming much more accessible, which was leading to a generation that had more opportunities to read and better access to books.

This history ties intrinsically to "Paperback Writer", simply because of the context: not only does the character in song want to be a writer, he wants to be a paperback writer because he knows deep down that writing a paperback book means that more people are going to have the opportunity to read it; in essence, knowing that his words are going to go farther in that format. Interestingly:

> Poet Royston Ellis, the first published author the Beatles had ever met when they played music backing his poetry in 1960, is convinced that Paul latched on to the phrase 'paperback writer' from his conversation with the group. 'Although I was writing poetry books then, if they asked me what I wanted to be I would always say a paperback writer because that's what you had to be if you wanted to reach a mass market' says Ellis (Turner, 2018, p. 152)

Regardless of his inspiration for the term, utilizing "Paperback Writer" specifically in the song is the first iconic sign we will discuss in this case study, as the specificity towards paperback writing brings up a historical reference that, without exploration, is lost. By exploring this history, we can begin to better understand the song in itself, and the ways in which it is intended to be understood.

Many people will recognize the Beatles through their incredible harmonies, which are globally revered. In fact, Walter Everett went so far as to provide a semiotic analysis of the ways in which harmony functions as an expressive device in She Loves You, to which he concludes: "the analysis of voice leading, with emphasis on harmony, register, and thematic design, thus yields not only serious discussion about black-and-white notes, but can also get to the heart of colourful musical expression, even that based in geniality, exuberance, and joy" (1993). With this in mind - that the Beatles' harmonies tend to express exuberance, joy, and general excitement - it becomes easy for us to realize exactly what kind of a sign the harmony is: for the Beatles, harmony exists as a symbolic sign, representing that unending excitement and exuberance. The fact that "Paperback Writer" begins with these harmonies means that the intention is to create excitement around the song before it even starts, and to return to that excitement every time the harmonies appear.

Not only that, the harmonies in "Paperback Writer" are inexact - some notes begin before others, as there are layers of vocals around the lyrics "Paperback Writer" at the beginning of the song, at the end of the song, and each time the phrase is repeated more than once. At the beginning, this can in part be attributed to the beginning being sung in acapella form, which is unusual for Beatles songs, but demonstrates the beauty of the harmonies all the same. Throughout the remainder of the song, the inexact harmonies provide a variety of listening points as listeners try to decipher whose voice is singing which line. Regardless, the harmonies in "Paperback Writer" function as symbolic signs, injecting excitement and enthusiasm into the song before it even starts, as well as throughout the song right until the very end.

The second, and possibly most interesting, sign in "Paperback Writer" takes the form of an indexical sign, and is hidden deeply enough in the song that many passive listeners never have the chance to pull it out and analyze it. The backing vocals for the song take the exact form of the childhood nursery rhyme Frère Jaques, which serves a variety of purposes. According to Steve Turner, "the background harmonies were inspired by the Beach Boys' album Pet Sounds [... and] during part of the harmonies [...] the Beatles can be heard singing 'Frère Jaques" as a subliminal exercise in evoking childhood memories" (2018, p. 152). While the Beach Boys were also a popular band at the same time as the Beatles, and their harmonies were also revered globally, the most interesting part about Turner's statement is about the use of Frère Jaques and its purpose: evoking childhood memories.

Remember back in chapter four, when we discussed the many ways in which music helps to evoke memories? This is simply one example of the ways in which this theory can be put to practical use. By putting Frère Jaques in the harmonies, the Beatles essentially hid the song out of sight, so that the lyrics would overshadow the childhood nursery rhyme. That said, hiding the song in the background doesn't mean it isn't there, so by including it, they utilized the connection between the nursery rhyme and memories of childhood in order to invoke those childhood memories during the playing of "Paperback Writer", which would theoretically create a stronger appeal to the song for certain people.

Whether or not these people would take the time to consider what it is that so actively draws them to "Paperback Writer", and why it is they seem to think of their childhood while listening to that song, is of no relevance: the important thing is that the Beatles included Frère Jaques in order to evoke those memories to help their listeners create a deeper bond with their song.

The final semiotic element in "Paperback Writer" that we will be discussing is that of the bass line, and the new technology of the time that was utilized to make it happen. "Paul was now playing a Rickenbacker and, through some studio innovations made by engineer Ken Townsend, the bass became the most prominent instrument on the track, bringing it into line with recent American recordings by Otis Redding and Wilson Pickett" (Turner, 2018, p. 152). Because the technology of the time had previously limited the ability to push bass lines to the forefront of recordings, being able to do so on "Paperback Writer" was a pleasant new innovation. Geoff Ererick speaks about the process of utilizing the bass line in such a way, saying that: "we boosted [the bass] further by using a loudspeaker as a microphone. We positioned it directly in front of the bass speaker and the moving diaphragm of the second speaker made the electric current" (Ererick, cited in Lewisohn, 1988, p. 74). By doing so, the recording was clear enough to be utilized in a lead instrument capacity and, according to Steve Turner, it was one of the first times the bass guitar had been used in such a way (2018, p. 152). By being innovative in this way, the Beatles found yet another way to bring new music to their listeners: not just new, but also with new and never-before-used technology, which allowed them to use the bass guitar in ways that hadn't been previously recorded.

As with every other case study we've taken on in this section, it's important for us to realize that we've really only scratched the surface considering the ways in which we can semiotically analyze "Paperback Writer". That said, we have covered some of the most important aspects, discussing form, instrumentation, the addition of childhood nursery rhymes, and the history behind some of the fascinating word choices within the song. By doing so, we now have a deeper understanding of why the song and story are so compelling to us, why we tend to think of our childhood when we listen to it, and why the lead bass guitar sounds so beautiful yet so innovative. At the same time, we have recognized the musical genius of the men who created this beautiful song for all to enjoy, and provided ourselves the opportunity to connect to the song on a deeper level, now that we know what semiotic mechanisms are in place to allow us to do so.

CONCLUSION

There are a wide variety of ways in which music communicates with us, and consequently, a wide variety of mechanisms to use to establish what music is trying to say and how it is doing so. This section on communication and music began by considering the expectations of musical form and musical signposting to consider some of the common ways in which composers lead their listeners on, so they have some instinctual idea of where the music will lead them next. We learned that in some cases, this signposting is built into pre-existing musical forms, and in other cases, it is used specifically to provide general direction for the listener so they can expect certain movement in the composition they are listening to. This introduction allowed us to delve into the meat and potatoes of the communication theory we were discussing: musical semiotics.

From the very introduction of musical semiotics, we learned that it is a multi-disciplinary and complicated theory that can take a wide variety of forms. We explored the ways that two theorists considered semiotics in general, and with the basis of that understanding, moved forth to musical semiotics, learning how the signs and symbols of semiotics can be seen, utilized, and understood in terms of music. From learning about the three common types of signs and how to deduce which aspects of our lives correspond to which signs to applying the signs to aspects of music and musical notation, we practically applied semiotics in general principle, which helped us gain a larger understanding of semiotics and musical semiotics as a whole.

Finally, we explored three different compositions in an attempt to utilize our understanding of musical semiotics and apply it in a practical manner. We considered Schubert's Erlkönig, for which the text was written by a poet and the music composed about the text; the fifth movement in Berlioz's Symphonie Fantastique, which was written by the composer himself with no words, only a story; and the Beatles "Paperback Writer," which is the only composition we studied that included both lyrics and music written by the composer. Through our analyses, we not only learned more about each specific song, but we also learned how to apply the logic of musical semiotics in a wide range of ways.

It is important to remember that musical semiotics is just one way of considering the ways in which music communicates to us; that said, it is an extremely practical and easy to understand way. With our knowledge, we will now be able to move forth both in life and in this book with the knowledge and skills to semiotically assess what a composition's purpose is, and how we, the listeners, are supposed to react to it. Let's keep this method of semiotic analysis in mind as we move into the next section in which we will discuss many more ways of thought about music and its purpose: through the minds of many great philosophers.

SECTION 4:
PHILOSOPHY

INTRODUCTION

Music has piqued the interest of many thinkers throughout the history of western philosophy. Unlike art forms such as paintings or sculptures, music has a mysterious invisibility. Since the ancients in Greece, philosophers have been known to emphasize the visible – what can be known and observed using our eyes (much of the same can be said of empirical scientists who, of course, overlap with philosophers, most certainly in pre-modern times). The challenge, then, is pinning down what exactly is going on in music and why it moves us in so many ways. Philosophical methods for understanding and attempting to answer these questions have varied significantly over the years. As we shall see, these methods range from the purely logical and mathematical to the purely spiritual and religious. And, though the conclusions that these thinkers come to may greatly and clearly be in conflict with one another, they all share and explain a certain truth about this mysterious art. It is the beauty of music, that human beings continue, time and time again, to return to music as a way to express something about the human experience of life on earth in seemingly infinitely unique ways that never cease to move us.

Our task in this chapter is to explore what western philosophers have to say about music, beginning with Plato and ending with Roger Scruton. Indirectly, there are two ways to realize the relationship between philosophy and music: either to a) explain something about music using philosophy or a philosophical method or b) to explain something about philosophy by using music, or an abstraction of a piece of music or musical method. For example, we might come to better understand Plato's logic in the Phaedo by exploring possible references to musical harmony (D. T. J. Bailey, 2005, 95–115). However, when speaking of music and philosophy, it is more common to think about a philosophy of music; that is, an aesthetic, or more generally, a philosophy of art. One can summarize generally the questions that a philosopher of art would ask in the following: What is music (in this era)? What makes for good music (or what makes music good)? What is music useful for? And, lastly, why do we like music? Of course, the last question is the one that has run through the entirety of this book.

Following the above lines of questioning, we shall first explore a history of ideas in western philosophy as they pertain to music. We will begin in ancient Greece, then move to the Medievals, followed thereafter by Modern philosophers, and finally, ending with the twentieth and the beginning of our twenty-first century. Along the way we will introduce and discuss key theories and explore how cultures and thought have evolved through time. By the end, you will have a broader and more in depth understanding of music and how it has interacted with western thought.

CHAPTER 11: ANCIENTS - PLATO, SOCRATES, AND ARISTOTLE

Plato (428/427 or 424/423 - 348/347 BC) and Socrates (470 - 399 BC)

It seems natural to begin our historical perusal of music and western philosophy with a discussion of Plato and his dialogues. For, although there are many ancients who came before him, Plato is truly the beginning of what has come to be known as philosophy today. Of course, Plato is not himself the voice in his dialogues. Instead, he writes through different voices, such as historical characters. Most famously, he writes through the voice of the philosopher, Socrates. It would be somewhat of a stretch to say that there is a great deal of discussion about music in Plato's works and, even within the little that is discussed about music, there is still much that is unknown regarding what music actually sounded like for the ancient Greeks. What we do know is that the Greek understanding of music heavily emphasizes the mathematical aspect of music. Proportionality, whether it be in reference to harmony, rhythm, or its poeticism, was central to good music. And those three main aspects, lyrics, mode or harmony, and rhythm were what was considered to make up good music.

Usually, and unsurprisingly, the poetry or words of the piece pertained to the occasion in which the music was performed. Music was performed at many occasions including festivals, parties, religious ceremonies, weddings, and funerals. Popular song types included hymns, paeans, prosodians, hyporchemas, and dithyrambs. Music was also known to accompany epic poetry, tragedies, and dramas. In fact, the name "music" comes from the Greek word "muses" who were the daughters of Zeus as well as the goddesses who inspired arts, literature, and science (Merriam-Webster, 2020). The mode of a piece of music expressed the mood of the piece, each mode represented a certain feeling, not unlike today's music. Certain modes invoked happy sentiments and others violent ones. Rhythm in Greek music was similar to the mode in that they also represented specific moods or feelings. Their rhythms were made of up two types, shorts and longs, where one long is equal, in proper proportion, to two shorts. The melody of a piece of music usually followed the words of the poetry closely in a syllabic style.

Now that we have a general sense of the music of ancient Greece, we might now ask what Plato brings to the discussion of music. To answer this question we must first look to Pythagorus and the Pythagoreans. Pythagorus claimed that music was a unique art that embodied the mathematical proportionality and harmony of the universe. He was the first to discover the relationship between notes that we now know as harmony. Pythagorus noticed that when you have a tensed string on an instrument, for example, and you divide that string in half, when you pluck those two strings they will be in harmony with one another; an octave, to be precise. A similar phenomenon happens with air column type instruments, and this is called an overtone or the overtone sequence. This idea is at the very foundation of music, and can all be explained mathematically. Pythagorus called this foundational phenomenon of universal harmony the "music of the spheres." These theories of Pythagorus were no doubt well known in Greece during Plato's lifetime and Plato no doubt subscribed to these notions in some way.

For Plato, music not only represented harmony, but was harmonious in and of itself. Music could represent the harmony of the universe and, in doing so, promote harmony within one's self. Music could therefore have subjective as well as intersubjective affects. This meant not only a harmony of one's own body and mind, but a harmony of one's entire life. Plato writes in the Protagoras "for the whole life of man stands in need of rhythm and harmony" (Plato, 2008, p. 326b). On this point Cornford notes that "this is not represented as a novel doctrine, but as if it were already a commonplace" (Plato, 1945, p. 88). Here we get a clearer glimpse at what Plato might understand as 'good' music; it is, interestingly enough, music that promotes the 'good.' Good music depends on a good character. Plato writes, through the voice of Socrates, "excellence of form and content in discourse and of musical expression and rhythm, and grace of form and movement, all depend on goodness of nature, by which I mean, not the foolish simplicity sometimes called by courtesy 'good nature', but a nature in which goodness of character has been well and truly established" (Plato, 1945, p.89). It seems that this can possibly mean two things. First, that good music can only be created by those who have a good character, and that musicians with good character are likely to make good music. Or, secondly, that it takes someone with good character to judge whether a piece of music is good. That someone with a good judgement, as part of their good character, will know and be wise to promote good music for the good of themselves and others. The second possibility seems like a stronger one, for not long after the above quote Plato's Socrates speaks of a certain type of perceptive judgement that recognizes good art from bad:

> [R]hythm and harmony sink deep into the recesses of the soul and take the strongest hold there, bringing the grace of the body and mind which is only to be found in one who is brought up in the right way. Moreover, a proper training in this kind makes a man quick to perceive any defect of ugliness in art or in nature... Approving all that is lovely, he will welcome it home with joy into his soul and, nourished thereby, he grows into a man of noble spirit (Plato, 1945, p. 90).

Music and the ability to judge, therefore, have a connection through the moral character. Exposure to music and the judging of music, then, is an important component of a good functioning society, which in Plato's world, was known as the polis.

It is evident, also, that Plato saw the study of music, or training in musical perception, as an important aspect of education for young students for, if they are able to judge music well, then those skills will transfer to life choices in the future. Plato's Socrates speaks to the importance of an education of this caliber stating, "the ultimate end of all education is insight into the harmonious order of the whole world" (Plato, 1945, pp.88-89). Aristotle, as we will see, takes on the concept of music education not long after.

Now, we have spoken of harmony, but we have not clarified exactly what might mean. Harmony, as we have alluded to already, had taken a large step forward with the work of Pythagorus. We see another great example of what harmony could mean, a definition that is not specifically musical but one that can have broader implications as well, in the dialogue the Symposium where, discussing the concept of love, Eryximachus claims:

> [I]n music there is the... reconciliation of opposites... [H]armony is composed of differing notes of higher or lower pitch which disagreed once, but are now reconciled by the art of music... For harmony is symphony, and symphony is an agreement; but an agreement of disagreements while they disagree cannot exist; there is no harmony of discord and disagreement. This may be illustrated by rhythm, which is composed of short and long, once differing and now in accord; which accordance... music implants, making love and unison to grow up among them: and thus music, too, is concerned with the principles of love in their application to harmony and rhythm (Plato, 1991, p. 187a-c).

Harmony, therefore, is something of an agreement or a reconciliation of opposites, where two sides that are seemingly in disagreement, come together to produce a pleasing sound. We observed a similar claim from Socrates, who stated that rhythm and harmony brought a grace to the body and mind, two apparently contradictory poles that come into agreement through this sort of harmony. To this end, Socrates concurs, "there can be no fairer sight than the harmonious union of a noble character in the soul with an outward form answering thereto and bearing the same stamp of beauty" (Plato, 1945, p. 91). Indeed, a human self is not only in need of a harmony with one's self, inside and out, but also to be in harmony with others and with the natural world.

We have examined the main components of music and how they relate to life in the polis, according to Plato. It is clear that music played a notable role in ancient Greek culture and that it had the potential for a significant influence as far as moral and personal characteristics are concerned. The Greeks used music for a variety of occasions, but Plato was most concerned with the quality of music and the effect it had on those that listened and participated in it. Plato saw the power of music and, though he did not write extensively about it, he showed its place in the universe. Taken on its face, music has the ability to move people, eliciting various emotions and expressing certain motivations. Analogically, music represents the possibility of harmony within oneself, oneself among others, and among the natural world. Let us now look to Aristotle to see how he continues Plato's thoughts on music.

ARISTOTLE (384 - 322 AD)

Aristotle's contribution to the philosophy of music, or music as it relates to human life, is that of a systemization of sorts. For if Plato's great ability is to narrativize or dialogize life's most difficult questions, then Aristotle's great ability was systemization. Aristotle created structures, themes, and rules that Plato's thought could be placed into and clarified. Not only that: he also had many critiques of Plato's work and is, therefore, certainly not merely a systematic thinker. The breadth of Aristotle's work reaches and touches upon in some way virtually every subject of inquiry. Being a student and contemporary of Plato, the music of Aristotle's time, we can safely say, is the same as that of Plato's. Aristotle, however, takes different emphases and, in many ways, clarifies what exactly Plato and the earlier ancients were attempting to say.

It might be appropriate, first, to have an understanding of Aristotle's works on the arts in general, which appear in various works, but most notably, in the Poetics and the Rhetoric. There are two important concepts that we can derive from these two works: mimesis, and katharsis.

Mimesis, out of which we get words like 'mimicry' and 'mime,' is a concept that speaks of art as an imitation, reflection, or representation of the natural world. Aristotle speaks of imitation as "natural to man from childhood, one of his advantages over the lower animals being this, that he is the most imitative creature in the world. And it is also natural for all to delight in works of imitation" (Aristotle, 2001, p. 1448b). Not only the ability to imitate other things, but also the desire to and pleasure in doing so, is something natural and unique to human beings, according to Aristotle. Poetry, argued Aristotle, is a form that imitates the natural world by representing narratives, aspects, and ideas from human life. The poets speak of heroes and conquerors, forests and flowers, myths and legends, some fantastical and some very real. This way of representing something of life somehow brings about pleasure for those who experience it. As Aristotle notes, "though the objects themselves may be painful to see, we delight in works of imitation" (Aristotle, 2001, p. 1448b).

That brings us to our second concept, katharsis, or, as it is more commonly known, catharsis. Katharsis is an effect of art that is the purgation or purification of emotions of pity and fear. A key trait of a work of tragedy, especially, is "incidents arousing pity and fear, wherewith accomplish its catharsis of such emotions" (Aristotle, 2001, p. 1449b). Today we understand catharsis in a somewhat similar way, where we have a final release of certain pent up emotions or feelings that, when expressed, give us a great amount of pleasure. Some people find action movies, like those of Bruce Lee, cathartic because of their controlled outburst of aggression; others look to a sad folk tune by Elliott Smith to express their fear of being alone. Interestingly enough, Aristotle, when he mentions the word 'katharsis' when referring to the works of tragedy, he speaks of "language with pleasurable accessories," by which he means "with rhythm and harmony or song superadded" when deemed appropriate.

So what, then, does Aristotle have to say about music? Along with Plato, Aristotle emphasizes the two of the key aspects that make up music: rhythm and harmony. This accounts not only for music as a substance, but also for music as a representation or a mimetic reflection of the natural world. Maybe the most telling statements of Aristotle are those found in Politics, for there we see exactly the purpose or end of music in his opinion. Here, he discusses the educational purpose of music, along with reading and writing, gymnastics, and sometimes drawing (Aristotle, 2001, p. 1337b). "Music" he claims, is "for intellectual enjoyment in leisure" which Aristotle states is "the reason for its introduction" (Aristotle, 2001, p. 1338a). This begs the question, why would it be beneficial to learn about music beginning at a young age if music is merely for the purpose of "intellectual enjoyment in leisure?"

In response, Aristotle states that music is good for not one, but three things: education, purgation, and intellectual enjoyment (Aristotle, 2001, p. 1341b). Simply put, music is necessary for a student's education because it teaches them "to become not only critics but also performers" for "it is difficult, if not impossible, for those who do not perform to be good judges of the performance of others" (Aristotle, 2001, p. 1340b). It seems that this maxim can apply not only to music, but also to a variety of life experiences in general. However, musical education is useful not only for judgment; it can also be useful for the sake of simply relaxing and enjoying music that is played, and that understanding can contribute to an enjoyment of the art. Regarding purgation, we can be fairly certain that with this term he means something along the same lines as our concept katharsis, for he speaks of this purgation in a very similar manner. In the following quote we can observe references to both katharsis and mimesis regarding music:

> Rhythm and melody supply imitations of anger and gentleness, and also of courage and temperance, and of all the qualities contrary to these, and of the other qualities of character, which hardly fall short of the actual affections, as we know from our own experience, for in listening to such strains our souls undergo a change (Aristotle, 2001, p. 1341a).

Music therefore has the ability to change a listener's character by its closeness to real life experience through a purgation of those pent up harmful emotions. Finally, music is considered to be "intellectual enjoyment" for it can amuse and relax those listeners as well. The tone and effect of the music often depends quite heavily on the mode that is used, and Aristotle makes this clear.

At the end of Politics, Aristotle discusses a disagreement that many have with the Socrates of the Republic. Socrates makes claim to a restricted number of musical modes that are appropriate for ethical music: Phyrigian and Dorian. But Aristotle states that Socrates is nearsighted with this claim. Aristotle argues to the contrary that "they ought to practice the gentler modes and melodies as well as the other" and to this end he makes specific reference to the Lydian mode for it "is suited to children of tender age, and possesses the elements of both order and of education" (Aristotle, 2001, p. 1342b).

In his summary, placed in the beginning table of contents for the book Politics, Aristotle summarizes concisely what is at the heart of his thought on music: "Music is taught as a recreation, but it serves a higher purpose. The noble employment of leisure is the highest aim which a man can pursue; and music is valuable for this purpose" (Aristotle, 2001, p. 1125). Aristotle differs from the Pythagorean and Platonic thought before him because of his much more practical thought about music. Music imitates the rhythm and harmony of the world, of the empirical world, and it has the ability to affect the behavior and character of those who hear it.

CHAPTER 12: MEDIEVALS – AUGUSTINE AND BOETHIUS

SAINT AUGUSTINE (354 - 430 AD)

We must now take a leap through time from the ancients in Greece to the medievals in northern Africa and Europe. With this leap comes not only the introduction of a different language, Latin, but also the introduction of a hugely influential and powerful institution: the Christian church. In Christianity we see a new perspective on music while still keeping many of the old Platonic and Aristotilian ideas. Because of the ubiquity of the Christian church in the west, the majority of the music created and performed was religious and created for the church; as Taruskin puts it, "it is both literally and figuratively service music: music for the divine service and music that serves a divine purpose" (Taruskin, 2005, p. 1). "Service music" dominated the music scene. The same can be said for much of the philosophical works at the time; that is, they combine Greek thought with the biblical tradition to form the amalgam that is medieval thought.

A large number of the philosophers that comprised this group of amalgamators were the Neo-Platonists.

"A Neoplatonist believed, first, that the world perceived by our sense organs was only a grosser reflection of a realer world, God's world, that we perceive with our God-given capacity for reasoning; and, second, that the purest form of reasoning was numerical reasoning, because it was least limited to what our senses tell us" (Taruskin, 2005, p.1). St. Augustine's thought, influenced by Neoplatonism, takes on some of these characteristics. However, one of the most influential works on music in the medieval era, his De Musica, has similar underlying themes as the work of Pythagorus. However, De Musica touches not on topics relating overtly to actual music or musical pieces, but only to rhythmic proportions. In this work we find his famous definition of music: "bene modulandi scientia or the art of measuring well" (Augustine, 1964, p. 191). Indeed, he often refers to music as the "rhythmic or metric art" (Augustine, 1964, p.189). According to Augustine, what makes for holy music is its composition of rhythm which is "immutable and eternal, with no inequality possible in it" (Augustine, 1964, p.190). Proportionality, measuredness, and equality are central elements of music that ascend beyond merely the senses to lead toward worship of God.

With a sense of a call to worship to the creator through song and voice comes also a strong inclination toward a Christian piety. Hence, there were a variety of restrictions that were put on music for it to be considered 'good' music, or music fit for worship. The central and most famous style of music during the time of both Augustine and Boethius (who we will discuss in the next section) was liturgical chant or hymn, which was composed of only voices because instrumental music or music that involved instruments was considered unfit for worship. Augustine writes, "sing and do not praise God, you do not utter a hymn. If you praise anything other than God, and if you sing these praises, still you do not utter a hymn. A hymn therefore has these three things: song, and praise, and God" (M. Gerbert, 2005, p. 74). It is clear that not only the content of the piece of music is important to its meaning, but also the intention and mindfulness of the participants.

Having thus mentioned this restrictedness, there remains no doubt that Augustine loved the music of his time. The beauty of the music in the church had him on many occasions swept away by its pleasurability. In his Confessions he writes:

> "I realize that all the varied emotions of the human spirit respond in ways proper to themselves to a singing voice and song, which arouse them by appealing to some secret affinity. Yet sensuous gratification, to which I must not yield my mind for fear it grow languid, often deceives me: not content to follow meekly in the wake of reason, in whose

company it has gained entrance, sensuous enjoyment often essays to run ahead and take the lead" (Augustine, 1997, p. 229).

Here we see Augustine's wonder at how the melody sung by the voice somehow has the ability to arouse a human response through one's emotions, done so through "some secret affinity." He then takes a step back to withdraw himself, for he must not be deceived by the sweet "sensuous gratification" of the music. To be taken up by a song for the sake of one's own pleasure is sin, but to glorify God through the substance of the text is praise. But we see that he finds himself often letting his enjoyment "take the lead" whereas a pious man would look to God rather than himself. It is reason, God given reason, that brings a mind back on the correct path. Taruskin writes that Augustine's "ambivalence ... has remained a characteristic of Western religious thinking about music" (2005, p. 2).

Yet, such ambivalence should not necessarily take away from the beauty of the music, for there is more to beautiful music than pleasing sounds. Augustine continues in The Confessions, again speaking to the power of the meanings given in the text:

> "I remember the tears I shed at the Church's song in the early days of my newly recovered faith, and how even today I am moved not by the singing as such but by the substance of what is sung, when it is rendered in a clear voice and in the most appropriate melodies, and then I recognize once more the value of this custom" (Augustine,1997, p. 230).

Here, he begins to put his finger on an important question in the world of music: which is more significant, the music or the text? It seems that Augustine emphasizes the importance of the text above the music - the meaning of the text is more important than the pleasure from the sounds; the music is meant to serve the text and not vice versa. However, we can no doubt see a personal struggle between his desire to be pious and his very human tendencies. He goes on: "thus I vacillate between the danger of sensuality and the undeniable benefits. Without pretending to give a definitive opinion I am more inclined to approve the custom of singing in church, to the end that through the pleasures of the ear a weaker mind may rise up to loving devotion" (p. 230). Augustine then concludes that, for the overall benefit of all who hear it, music should remain in the church, even though its beauty may distract the listeners from its holy creator, God.

Although in his more personal work, The Confessions, we find in Augustine a love but also a struggle when it comes to the practical art of music, in his truly philosophical thinking he has no concern for the actual music heard. He tends to rather focus centrally on the harmony and rhythm of the cosmos and its relation to God and human beings. At the root of the beauty in music still remains rhythm and harmony. He writes succinctly, "[E]arthly things are subject to heavenly things, seeming to associate the cycles of their own durations in rhythmic succession with the song of the great whole, universitatis" (Augustine, 1997, p.186). Although this thought is not far from statements made by Pythagorus and Plato, where Augustine differs from those previous two thinkers is in his Christian foundation. Harmony and rhythm, the way in which music unites us to the natural world, is taken one step further: it brings the listener closer to knowing God and understanding the nature of the universe.

A. M. S. Boethius (477 - 524 AD)

When it comes to actual output regarding the topic of music, compared to the vast majority of medieval thinkers, Boethius has quite a substantial amount of work in the field. However - and this is likely true of all the thinkers we have discussed thus far - he did not know much about actual musical practice; for example, how to play an instrument or sing proficiently. But, given his context, this is neither unusual nor surprising, for it displays the common worldview in his time. Boethius' work laid the groundwork for what we understand as today's music theory, and his work on the topic of music was focused mainly in that area - music theory. Like Augustine, Boethius was heavily influenced, not only by Pythagorus and the Pythargoreans, but also by the Neoplatonists. He held onto those common ideas from both groups: that music reflected the harmony and rhythm of the cosmos, and that it influenced humans and their behaviour.

Boethius' primary and most notable philosophical addition to thought about music comes in his De Institutione Musica, where we find his division of the different types of what he calls "Musica," which puts a name to the harmony and rhythm of the spheres (think Pythagorus).

There are three divisions of Musica: Musica mundana, Musica humana, and Musica instrumentalis (Taruskin, 2005, p. 1).

The first, Musica mundana, represents the harmony of the cosmos. This includes the four elements, (earth, wind, fire, and water) the four seasons and their continuing cycle, the sun and the moon which equate to the day and the night, and all the celestial bodies in the sky. Regarding the seasons he writes: "for that which winter binds, spring releases, summer scorches and autumn ripens, and in turn the seasons themselves either produce their own fruits or aid others to produce" (Boethius, 1985, p. 133). There is observably a natural balance between the opposite forces in the world that one never overpowers another to an extreme, but that they always find their proper proportion and equilibrium. These natural movements, seemingly written into the fabric of the universe, Boethius calls "musical." As Boethius states, "whence the fixed order of the musical modulation cannot fail to result from this celestial revolution" (1985, p.133).

Below Musica mundana is Musica humana, the music of human beings. However, this is not the musical sounds that we create, even if it is naturally; instead, it is the harmony with one's own being and one's own self. This harmony is made up of the proper proportions of what were known as the humors, which date back to the ancient Greeks. There are four humors that make up a human being, once thought to be real biological characteristics of humans, which correspond to the four seasons and the four elements: blood/sanguine (spring/air), yellow bile/choleric (summer/fire), black bile/melancholic (autumn/earth), phlegm/phlegmatic (winter/water) (Taruskin, 2005, p. 3). Human music is naturally introspective, and one can discover it simply by reflecting on human kind. To this end Boethius writes, "whoever turns his attention to his own self understands human music (Boethius, 1985, p. 133).

The final and lowest form of Musica is Musica instrumentalis, which is the actual, audible music made by musical instruments. This not only includes instruments such as the cithara and the flute, but also the voice. Within the category of audible music, Boethius designates different possible roles that one could play: "there are three genera which are concerned with the musical art: one kind uses instruments, another invents songs, and the third judges the performance of instruments and the songs" (p. 153). It is interesting to note his clear division of these three, to which today we would not demarcate so clearly. Boethius states that the first two designations are not truly musicians because they do not use their reason or speculative powers in order to fulfill their tasks, where as the expert judge "applies himself completely to reason and speculation" and therefore, "he is the one who is properly called [a] musician" (p. 153-154). If his assessment of the musician was not clear enough, he caps it off by stating: "how much more honorable is therefore the science of music in the speculation of the mind than in the labor of producing and the mere action" (p.153)

De Institutione Musica also, and for the most part, features theoretical work regarding the physics of sound and mathematics. Here we find the beginnings of the diatonic, chromatic, and enharmonic scales, which are made up of tetrachords, in which are notes with varying pitch spaces between them depending on the scale. Using intervals from Pythagorean thought, the octave (1:2), the fifth (2:3), and the fourth (3:4), Boethius shows how, by combining any two of those ratios, other intervals will arise from those fundamental intervals. He then takes all the possible combinations and designates them each with a name. He also gives a definition of sound that goes as follows: "a percussion of the air which is undissolved even to the hearing" (p. 134). By "undissolved" he appears to mean retaining its form, or not dissipating before it hits the ear. Sadly, a large portion of this work has been lost, and only the first book and part of the second book of this work were conserved.

Boethius contributed a significant amount to not only the history of the philosophy of music, but also to the history of music in general. Known in part for his systematicity, he organized, progressed, and developed the culmination of work that began with Pythagorus. Aside from his notable benefaction to music, physics, and theory, he also incorporated novel abstract ideas about music and how it relates to the three fundamental aspects of the universe in his division of Musica. Boethius' work helped and still helps many generations understand the fundamentals of music found in and originating from Greek thought.

CHAPTER 13:
MODERNS - KANT
AND SCHOPENHAUER

IMMANUEL KANT (1724 - 1804)

From the medievals we take another monumental leap (about 1200 years) to what is considered the modern era of western philosophy. Immanuel Kant's work essentially denotes the end of the enlightenment movement, as he marks the "Copernican revolution" in the history of philosophy. To get an idea of the music of Kant's day, he was a contemporary of Haydn (1732 - 1809), Mozart (1756 - 1791), and Beethoven (1770 - 1827). It's possible that Kant would be aware of at least Haydn or Mozart, although Königsberg, Prussia, where Kant spent the majority of his life, is quite distant from where these composers spent their time. Of course, to touch on everything that we have leaped over from the middle ages would be impossible, so we will remain focused on the novel concepts and ideas that Kant brings to the discussion of music and philosophy.

To begin with, Kant had an enormously greater interest in actual audible music, or sensations, than any other thinker that we have talked about thus far, a fact that can mostly be attributed to the many huge cultural shifts spanning the time between Boethius and Kant. He also has a much wider interest in music beyond the purely mathematical and proportional properties, and rather considers the emotional and rational judgement of music to be of the utmost importance. His central work pertaining to music and the arts in general is the Critique of Judgement, which considers the analytic of the beautiful and the human capacity for judgement, amongst other topics. The question of the beautiful, though it is certainly present in the works of the thinkers we have discussed, has not been for us an important topic in relation to music as we have encountered it so far. For Kant, however, the nature of beauty is a key question in relation to the arts. This question is also an important one as it relates directly to our overarching question of why we like music.

To help us understand beauty in music according to Kant, it will be helpful to lay out his division of fine art. He first defines fine art as "a way of presenting that is purposive on its own and that furthers, even though without a purpose, the culture of our mental powers to [facilitate] social communication" (p.173). Kant then divides fine art into three categories based on thought, intuition, and sensation; hence, correspondingly, the art of speech, visual art, and the art of the play of sensations (Kant, 1987, p. 190). Within the art of speech there is oratory and poetry. Next, within the visual arts, there are forms like sculpture and architecture (plastic arts), and painting proper and landscape gardening (painting arts). What makes the visual arts different from the art of speech is that it "expresses ideas in sensible intuition" rather than "mere imagination... by words" (Kant, 1987, p.191). Lastly, there is the art of the beautiful play of sensations, which is divided into sensations of hearing and sight, music, and the art of colour (Kant, 1987, p.193). Kant claims that music and the art of colour are the most difficult arts to judge aesthetically because it is often uncertain whether we experience them as merely agreeable sensation or as a beautiful play of sensation and hence a liking for its form (1987, p.194). Regarding this difficulty, Kant considers two things: the judging of their mathematical ratio, and the fact that even the most prodigious and sensitive listeners and observers have trouble making finer distinctions between certain tones and certain colours. Since there seems to be such a limit, "we may feel compelled to regard sensation of colour and tone not as mere sense impressions, but as the effect of our judging of the form we find in the play of many sensations" (Kant, 1987, p.194).

The questions 1) whether music is beautiful, and 2) why we like music, are two distinct, though not unconnected questions. Let us first look at some of the answers Kant gives for the second question so we can then address the first question. One reason that we have a liking for music is that its tone and rhythmic sounds, in a sense, have a parallel to the voice in speech. He writes:

[Music's] charm, so generally communicable, seems to rest on this: Every linguistic expression has in its context a tone appropriate to its meaning. This tone indicates, more or less, an affect of the speaker and in turn induces the same affect in the listener too, where it then conversely arouses the idea which in language we express in that tone" (Kant, 1987, p.198).

Another reason that we like music, in strict contrast with many in the history of the philosophy of music, is not because of the mathematics of music, for "mathematics certainly does not play the slightest part in the charm and mental agitation that music produces," but it is a matter of the ratio of continuous affective impressions which creates an "agitation and quickening of the mind, and thus they produce an appealing self-enjoyment" (Kant, 1987, p. 199). By "mental agitation" Kant means "what emotion involves" or a stirring of emotion, and by "quickening of the mind" he denotes an intellectual cognizing of the presentation of the music. But the essential reason that we like music is because it presents sounds in a charming, agreeable, or beautiful way and therefore is aesthetic.

For Kant, charm, the agreeable, and beauty are three distinct concepts. Charm, defined by a certain niceness or surface level pleasurability, is one of the main features of the agreeable arts; the "agreeable arts are those whose purpose is merely enjoyment" (Kant, 1987, p. 172). Our first question, asked above, relates music to the third concept, beauty. Kant states that "[w]e may in general call beauty (whether natural or artistic) the expression of aesthetic ideas" (1987, p.189), and, more specifically, "[a] rtistic beauty is a beautiful presentation of a thing" (1987, p. 179). Kant concluded then that the determination of beauty arises from a subject's taste, claiming, first that "[t]aste is the ability to judge an object, or a way of presenting it, by means of a liking or disliking devoid of all interest," and that therefore, "[t]he object of such a liking is called beautiful" (1987, p. 53).

Can music be beautiful then? Kant seems to claim that it depends on certain criteria. First, it depends on the quality of the listener's judgement. As we mentioned, the judgement has to be "devoid of all interest", meaning that the listener must be "indifferent to the existence of the object" (Kant, 1987, p. 51). Second, it depends on the situation. The listener must be listening cognitively and consciously to the music, rather than the music being pleasing background sounds. Lastly, of course, the music must fit the criteria of fine art, that is, a presentation of an aesthetic idea without a concept.

To conclude, Kant puts his definition and his thought about music quite concisely when he states that music is "a language of affects" (1987, p. 199). Music has the ability to ignite a person's cognitive faculties in a way that not only stimulates emotion, but also produces pleasure. However, not every piece of music has the intellectual qualities that Kant sees as necessary for a beautiful work of fine art: some pieces of music are simply charming and useful as a social lubricant, for example. Kant shows that, of the fine arts, music is a unique and often difficult form to pin down or thoroughly categorize. Much of the judgement of a piece of music is contextual, and yet, for Kant, this does not take away from one's ability to make a universal claim to music's beauty.

ARTHUR SCHOPENHAUER (1788 - 1860)

Schopenhauer's philosophical thought regarding music is a unique one in the histories of both western philosophy and western music. Few philosophers have integrated music into their work on such a serious and critical level. Building off of the monumental groundwork of Kant, he paved a unique path, one very distinct in many ways from that of Kant. He is the first of the thinkers that we have examined thus far to take an outright atheistic approach, and is well-known as one of the chief philosophers of pessimism in western thought. Composer Richard Wagner (1813 - 1883) took great interest in Schopenhauer's work, as did Schopenhauer in Wagner's work, as they shared various common interests, and works of Wagner's such as Der Ring des Nibelungen have been influenced by Schopenhauer's thought.

To understand Schopenhauer's thoughts on music, we must first discuss the central tenets of his philosophy. In the first sentence of his work The World as Will and Representation he writes, "The world is my representation" (Schopenhauer, 1969, p. 3). The world, then, is received subjectively through our senses, through our sensory organs, rather than pure and unmediated. The other side of this coin is the world-in-itself, or the objective world - this is the world as will. For Schopenhauer, the will, manifested in human beings, results in infinite and eternal dissatisfaction. He states: "now the nature of man consists in the fact that his will strives, is satisfied, strives anew, and so on and on; in fact his happiness and well-being consist only in the transition from desire to satisfaction, and from this to a fresh desire, such transition going forward rapidly" (1969, p. 260). A human being's acts are never free, but are always subject to their own will, which one can never fully control: one's will does as it pleases. This is the fundamental reason, according to Schopenhauer, that people suffer, and that suffering is inevitable and unavoidable.

However, one sure, albeit temporary, release from the grips of the will is through the experience of art, or aesthetic contemplation. In these moments of contemplation the observer loses themselves in the artwork and becomes immersed in the experience. The object of the art begins to appear in a different way than in everyday life: the observed begins to lose grips on the hard line between themselves and the object. For Schopenhauer, music is the most effective and most conducive medium for this experience, because there is no clear real object in music; that is it is the most abstract, and that it did not merely copy the things of the world but was something entirely unique. Schopenhauer writes:

> [Music] stands quite apart from all the others. In it we do not recognize the copy, the repetition, of any Idea of the inner nature of the world. Yet it is such a great and exceedingly fine art, its effect on man's innermost nature is so powerful, and it is so completely and profoundly understood by him in his innermost being as an entirely universal language, whose distinctness surpasses even that of the world of perception itself (1969, p. 256).

While other arts are merely copies of other objects or concepts in the world - even the most abstract like beauty or goodness - music goes even deeper to the most fundamental concept in the world: the will itself.

> Therefore music is by no means like the other arts, namely a copy of the Ideas, but a copy of the will itself, the objectivity of which are the Ideas. For this reason the effect of music is so very much more powerful and penetrating than is that of the other arts, for these others speak only of the shadow, but music of the essence (Schopenhauer, 1969, p. 257).

If music truly gets to the very core of being - that music is a copy of the will - then, Schopenhauer claims, the reverse is also true, that in a certain sense the world itself is embodied music.

Schopenhauer claims that because of the nature of music and its meaning in the world it acts as a universal language that is understood, known, and appreciated in some capacity by all people:

> As a result of all this, we can regard the phenomenal world, or nature, and music as two different expressions of the same thing; and this thing itself is therefore the only medium of their analogy, a knowledge of which is required if we are to understand that analogy. Accordingly, music, if regarded as an expression of the world, is in the highest degree a universal language that is related to the universality of concepts much as these are related to the particular things (1969, p. 262).

One might ask, then, does music represent everything of the world, even the smallest banalities to the most mundane parts of life? Schopenhauer claims that it is not that there is music for every minute aspect of life or even that the mathematical proportions of music are in harmony with ourselves and the universe. Rather, he states: "Everywhere music expresses only the quintessence of life and of its events, never these themselves, and therefore their differences do not always influence it. It is just this universality that belongs uniquely to music, together with the most precise distinctness, that gives it that high value as the panacea of all our sorrows" (p. 261 - 262). Within the category of music, there remains smaller categorizations that differentiate between more and less effective works. Schopenhauer states the music that maintains its own language - the language of music - rather than following the language of speech, is the one that is most effective, for it stays true to the nature of the world and does not drift into the world of objects. He claims that the one composer who epitomizes this idea is Gioachino Rossini (1792 - 1868).

To put his thoughts on music and its relation not only to other arts but to human beings and the world quite succinctly, he summarizes it by writing:

> That in some sense music must be related to the world as the depiction to the thing depicted, as the copy to the original, we can infer from the analogy with the remaining arts, to all of which this character is peculiar; from their effect on us, it can be inferred that that of music is on the whole of the same nature, only stronger, more rapid, more necessary and infallible. Further, its imitative reference to the world must be very profound, infinitely true, and really striking, since it is

148

instantly understood by everyone, and presents a certain infallibility by the fact that its form can be reduced to quite definite rules expressible in numbers, from which it cannot possibly depart without entirely ceasing to be music (1969, p. 256).

In conclusion, Schopenhauer's thought relies more heavily on the art of music, likely more than any other thinker in western philosophy. His pursuit in examining and displaying the unique power of music is one that few have matched. We saw that music has the potential to relieve the listener of the burden of their will: their daily desires and the banality of everyday life. Music is attributed this power because of its ability to cut to the very core of existence and take the listener to the very heart of life; it bridges the gap between the otherworldly and the self.

CHAPTER 14:
20TH CENTURY TO
PRESENT - ADORNO
AND SCRUTON

THEODOR W. ADORNO (1903 - 1969)

Although from the end of our so-called modern era to this final era in our discussion of the history of philosophy and music there stands the smallest gap thus far, between these two eras marks a great many differences. These differences are no doubt in part due to the major worldwide historical events that take place in the 20th century, which of course includes two world wars. Adorno also certainly writes and thinks in response to these major historical events. He is another thinker that takes music very seriously and works musical thought into his work often, with the inclusion of many works with music as its central topic. Adorno himself was a skilled musician and composed a number of pieces of music. Additionally, Adorno's thoughts on music are likely some of the most controversial in the history of music and philosophy, and many have written him off as inconsequential because of a vast array of disagreements with his thought. But that should not dissuade us from discussing these ideas, for the thoughts he puts forth remain influential in the world of music to this day.

Often Adorno's social theories and principles are transposed into his thoughts about music. It may be helpful, first, to get an idea of where his thought can be categorized within the history of philosophy in order to see the relation between his musical works and his other work.

Adorno was part of what was known as the Frankfurt School, which included other members such as Walter Benjamin (1892 - 1940) and Max Horkheimer (1895 - 1973), who had a critical approach to social theory called critical theory. These theories were founded on the works of thinkers like G. W. F. Hegel (1770 - 1831), Sigmund Freud (1856 - 1939), and Karl Marx (1818 - 1883), and specifically critiqued themes in culture and politics. Adorno took special interest in themes like ideology, anti-fascism, and anti-totalitarianism, and was quite critical of popular culture, particularly art in pop culture. This particular interest in the theory of art can be summarized as follows:"He preserves the notion of the artwork as a more or less integral text that inscribes the social in its internal relations and serves as a medium for reflecting the true social condition of the subject" (Witkin, 2000, p. 149 - 150).

For Adorno, an ideal piece of music treats musical notes, themes, and ideas like the subjects in an ideal society. The notes in their mutual, spontaneous, dialectical interaction is what dictates the structuration of the piece: what drives and pushes the piece forward, the same as in society where mutual relations between people are the central drive. The drive should not come from a heavily restrictive structure that removes spontaneity and freedom, nor should it entirely arise out of specific preconceived notions about the capacity for certain musical elements. Witkin writes:

> It does so from below, from the free and sponta- neous development of the musical elements in their mutual relations and not from above, by the imposition of a transcendental form or order upon them" and that "it is the all-important process of mediation and change among the elements (notes) that constructs temporality and historicity in the music" (2000, 148).

Musical ideas develop, not on their own individually nor coincidentally, but out of and off of each other, mutually. The notes, ideas, or motives are treated as developing live subjects who interact and play with the others to develop organically. Adorno, therefore, emphasizes the work itself, rather than the composer or reliance on previous works and styles.

This ideal - this "principle of structuration" - is one of the underlying reasons for his criticism of popular music, and specifically jazz (Witkin, 2000, p.148). According to Adorno, jazz as a genre (which he categorized quite broadly on many occasions) does not have within it any real dialectical development substance, but rather merely uses ornamentation to create the illusion of development. Its structure is conducive, not to spontaneity of a progressive end, but to a circular and redundant end. Adorno much preferred the avant-garde classical style to any other style. A second, not entirely unrelated, reason that Adorno disliked jazz was because it promoted a capitalist culture industry. He claims that, because of its inability to promote structural newness or progress, it does not provide any valuable material to the musical world and is therefore merely agreeable. It, too, is a problem because of its commercialization and fetishization, indeed, "fetishism takes hold of even the ostensibly serious practice of music, which mobilizes the pathos of distance against refined entertainment" (Adorno, 2001, p. 44). Jazz, and also popular music in general, promote content that feeds on commerciality instead of artistic innovation.

Adorno's specified logic applied to jazz and popular music can, in a somewhat similar way, be applied to his criticism of the work of Igor Stravinsky (1882 - 1971) as well. Stravinsky and his contemporary Arnold Schoenberg (1874 - 1951) represented two main streams in classical music after the turn of the century. While Schoenberg's style was quite avant-garde and experimental in many ways with his atonal and twelve-tone works, Stravinsky's style was returned to the fundamentals of classicism with his innovations in rhythmic structuring. Adorno criticized Stravinsky's signature use of rhythm and meter, particularly in his Neo-classical period, for being regressive. Stravinsky's return to previous forms rather than new and progressive styles, and his focus on the old form rather than the liberation of musical ideas to be organic, accumulated in a critical review from Adorno. Schoenberg, on the other hand, was championed by Adorno, and he often praised him for his "compositional developments of tonality" (Gracyk, 1992, p. 535). Where Adorno saw musical brilliance in much of the work of Schoenberg, he did not so much see it in Stravinsky.

Though much of his thought on music has been deemed inconsequential by many (on Adorno, Taruskin wrote that he is "preposterously over-rated" (2005, p. xiv)), that should not deny us a brief discussion of his relationship with western music, nor should we immediately write him off, for even in his controversy he has something to offer. He very much took music as an art very seriously, even if he often had a fairly narrow conception of what constituted real music. Few mainstream philosophers have taken to task musicology and thought on music to the extent that Adorno did.

ROGER SCRUTON (1944 - 2020)

Aesthetics was a central line of work for Scruton, who published his first book, Art and Imagination, based on his PhD thesis on said topic. Besides aesthetics, his other interest was political philosophy, specifically writing on conservatism. One central theme in his work on art is the recovery of the concept of beauty, which in the past hundred years or so has become quite unpopular. His inscription to the "A Very Short Introduction Series" called Beauty: A Very Short Introduction speaks to attempts at reexamining beauty. Similar to his thought on beauty, his thought about music is critical and yet offers many inclusive and expansive pathways for the art.

One aspect that Scruton finds unique and interesting about music is its abstract nature in the sense that, perceptually, we do not experience the object of music. He writes in his book Understanding Music,

> Sounds ... can be identified without referring to any object which participates in them, and it is precisely this feature that is seized upon by music, and made into the template on which the art of music is built. Because sounds are pure events we can detach them, in thought and experience, from their causes, and impose upon them an order that is quite independent of any physical order in the world" (Scruton, 2009, p. 5).

That experience, the sort of unmediated nature of music, Scruton calls the "acousmatic experience" (2009, p. 5). We never hear the "object" of sound (the physical sound waves) but we experience what they mean or what they signify; there is not the same mediating process that there is in, say, a painting. Scruton writes, "sounds heard as music are heard in abstraction from their physical causes and effects, and assembled in another way, as individuals in a figurative space of their own" (2009, p. 7).

Scruton realizes the interpretative and strictly human nature of music. There is no music apart from the human beings who make it and the humans who listen to it. There is no "music" that is innate to the world or pre-human music. For music to be heard, it must be heard as music and not simply a combination or assortment of sounds. This implies a rational mind that can organize and deliberate about music. Scruton writes, "Music exists when rhythmic, melodic or harmonic order is deliberately created, and consciously listened to, and it is only language-using, self-conscious creatures, I argue, who are capable of organizing sounds in this way, either when uttering them or when perceiving them" (p.6). A bird, for example, does not understand their song as "song" in the same way that a human would organize those same sounds and understand it as music.

Music therefore also necessitates a certain pre-understanding of what you are listening to. We must be able to recognize a musical experience from a non-musical one. "Music relies neither on linguistic order nor on physical context, but on organization that can be perceived in sound itself, without reference to context or to semantic conventions" (p.5). This means that, although the aspects of linguistic order and physical context affect music, music does not rely on these traits to convey musical meaning to the listener; music as organized sound can be meaningful in itself. And we already have an understanding of musical meaning in the form of a certain innate ability for aesthetic experiences. "Musical meaning is not established by convention, assigning meanings to musical objects in the manner of a code of semaphore signals. The meaning of a work of music is given only in the aesthetic experience, and is not available simply by applying rules" (p.50). Scruton's emphasis is, therefore, more on the experience of music on the side of the listener than the object of music on the side of the conventional "piece" or "work".

Regarding the historical question of the "natural" nature of music, one that we have explored through various thinkers, Scruton is sceptical of a quick resolve to the Pythagorean way of natural harmony (2009, p. 13). Of course, this is not that it is without truth. But one can too easily fall back on the mathematical claim to a universal liking of music. Scruton claims that there still involves the need for human organization and intention: "The 'natural' relations among tones are at best raw material, from which scales, modes and harmonic devices emerge by habit and experiment. The order that we learn to hear is permeated by the traditions that have shaped our ears. And these traditions vary from culture to culture..." (2009, p. 14).

Another central idea for Scruton concerning the musical experience is the importance of listening. He writes, "even if there are sound ethnological reasons for believing that music originated in dance and song, listening, I maintain, is the heart of all musical cultures. You cannot sing or dance if you do not listen to the music that you are singing or dancing to" (p. 12). Although this claim may be simple, it is often overlooked. From an economic perspective, music can become suffocated by commodification, and the consumer often turns from listening to music to merely hearing it, which slowly drains styles and pieces of their uniqueness, individuality, and their meaning. A dialectical approach to music listening opens up possibilities for innovation, but also a deeper appreciation for the art and simply creates a better aesthetic experience.

Truly listening to music opens the listener up to the expressive intersubjective nature of music. Scruton claims:

> When you move to music, the music takes charge of your response to it—you are being led by it, from gesture to gesture, and each new departure is dictated by the musical development. You are not merely noticing analogies between the movement of the music and some state of mind: you are entering into dialogue with it, fitting your own emotions to the rhythm that it conveys, as you might when experimenting with inter-personal sympathies, and coming to understand both self and other more completely" (2009, p. 55).

A sympathetic or empathetic response to music is natural, for music is meant to be shared.

To conclude, Scruton's careful analysis of musical perception and our experience of music is one of the more nuanced discussions to date. With the proliferation of styles and genres in our current globalized world, one must be keenly aware of a broad range of musical perspectives in order to have a proper understanding and a proper critique. Scruton was able to meet these changing conditions and did so quite well. It is clear that he had a sincere appreciation for the art of music and worked to expand and improve musical thought in order for it to be appreciated on a wider scale and a deeper level.

CONCLUSION

Throughout our exploration of philosophical thought and how it relates to music, we have examined a great variety of perspectives, all who, in one way or another, had a deep connection to the art of music. It is clear that music has been an important part of western thought and has accompanied the many thinkers throughout the history of the west. We began with the ancients in Greece, who, influenced by the great work of Pythagorus, took up both practical and metaphysical responses to music. The medievals, with the introduction of Christianity, had a fresh take on Greek thought, discussing personal and systematic philosophical theories. Next, we saw that modernity brought both a deeply rational, but also truly existential perspective to musical thought, showing its place within the world of thought and within the concrete world. Finally, the contemporary thought of the 20th and 21st centuries brought us up to date with their contrasting specific and narrow theories and broad, nuanced thought.

We have asked many questions - ones that are common to an exploration of the aesthetics of music such as this - and we have discussed a wide range of answers to these questions. Some final, still unanswered questions yet remain. Can music be called the language of emotions? Is the language we use to describe and define music specific to our western perspective, to our specific ideologies? What is the nature of our seemingly universal ability to have these aesthetic experiences? With our ever expanding circles of influence in this globalized world, will "western thought" and "western music" become a thing of the past? The quest for an understanding of music is not one that is ever finished, but is an endless discussion with infinite nuances and pathways. Our discussions show, in a fascinating manner, the ability for the same questions to persist for generations, with thinkers from all over converging on these important matters.

SECTION 5: POLITICS

INTRODUCTION

Humans are social creatures. In the earlier section on biology, we discussed how music evolved as a form of communication. This evolution facilitated the development of more advanced societies, which in turn produced more advanced music. This feedback loop is ongoing, and can be seen through an examination of music and politics.

Like language or food, music is a definitive aspect of almost every culture around the world. We are often able to immediately determine the origin of music we hear by its unique sound. When we hear flamenco music, we associate it with Spain; when we hear mariachi music, we associate it with Mexico; when we hear country music, we associate it with the American South. Of course, these are not hard and fast rules; music, like food or language, can spread out from its original culture to other cultures and become inculcated in those cultures' identities. Even the examples above trace their beginnings to multiple other cultures, such as how flamenco music has influences from Arab culture.

There is not one single way to understand politics, just as there is not one single way to understand music. To some, politics is little more than the art of backstabbing, or it is the backroom deals where decisions are made. Deserved or not, politics is often used as a derogatory term. For example, someone might complain that they "love their job but hate the politics of it." What this person dislikes - what they have termed 'politics' - is how their job is dominated by the petty power of interpersonal favours and favourites.

This is not the sort of politics being referred to in this section. Here, politics will refer to the system(s) of governance a society has developed to organize itself. An important point is that these are systems - they are larger than one person - but they are inhabited by individuals. Politics in this sense plays a large role in shaping the culture of the society it is governing while at the same time being a product of that culture.

To clarify, think of a game or a sport. These can be developed deliberately or they can develop organically. As the game is played, rules are added or removed in order to improve the game. These rules shape the game, but the game also shapes the rules. Of course, the complex issue is what could be called the essence of the game; that understanding of what the game truly is or should be. This is the same issue that arises in politics all the time: what are the true values of our society? What is our society's essence?

The relationship between music and politics may be difficult to see at first, which returns us to the feedback loop. The societies we live in produce music, and they produce music for many different reasons. One of the most vital functions music fulfills - perhaps its original function - is its ability to communicate in a unique way. Sometimes there is nothing besides music that can convey the exact message or mood someone wants to convey. And there is nothing like music that allows large amounts of people to experience this mood or message together. Music can capture essence.

The capturing of essence through music is a powerful political tool. If we understand politics as the governance of a society, then it is important for those engaging in politics to be able to communicate with those they wish to govern. And those who are governed often find music as the best way to express themselves. Therefore music often finds itself a battleground of political messages.

With a deep and rich history that stretches back before historical memory, the relationship between music and politics could be illustrated by innumerable examples. For this book, examples from American history have been chosen, and even then, there is too much history to discuss them all. From the cheerful satire of "Yankee Doodle" in America's earliest days to Jazz in the 1920s to the music of the counterculture revolution of the 1960s to today, there are thousands of songs, movements, artists, and genres that would work perfectly well as examples.

The examples that have been chosen will make up the subsequent chapters. They will build upon each other in an attempt to fully demonstrate the complex relationship between music and politics. The first of these chapters will centre on America's national anthem, the "Star Spangled Banner." The second will focus on a different sort of anthem - the so-called anthem of the Civil Rights movement, "We Shall Overcome." Lastly, we shall critically examine the play "Hamilton", a musical hip-hop reimagining of America's earliest decades.

CHAPTER 15:
THE ANTHEM

Every nation has symbols chosen to represent itself. The most powerful, popular symbols are usually the flag and the anthem, which are often heavily associated with each other. It is not a coincidence that the anthem has become one of the primary symbols of national identity around the world. Regardless of culture, the underlying properties of music, rooted deep in our evolutionary history as a species, are naturally suited to bringing diverse groups of people together. The anthem is the perfect encapsulation of the relationship between music and politics.

Music allows us to communicate wordlessly; or, in the anthem's case, allows us to communicate through solidarity. The lyrics are sung by everyone simultaneously, an effect that draws people together in common cause through common action. Ideally, you and your fellow anthem singers are able to touch upon some of the same emotions of reverence and respect and connect because of those shared emotions, even when you do not share anything else. By mixing in the flag, you have a potent ritual that takes advantage of our natural tendencies to communicate through music and symbols, as our societies have done for millenia.

This is especially true in America, where the anthem is about the flag, the "Star Spangled Banner." In fact, the very flag that inspired the author of the "Star Spangled Banner" still exists, safely cared for in the Smithsonian museum (Lineberry, 2007). America reveres its flag and anthem, which is not an accident - it is a piece of music designed to be a cultural symbol that is supposed to represent the essence of America. By definition, opinions on the anthem are inherently political.

A SHORT HISTORY OF THE "STAR SPANGLED BANNER"

The "Star Spangled Banner" originally had a different title: "Defence of Fort M'Henry" (Lineberry, 2007). It was written by Francis Scott Key on September 14, 1814, as he watched the fort survive an overnight bombardment from British forces during the War of 1812 (Lineberry, 2007). The poem was set to the tune of a popular song, as was common practice at the time, and distributed by newspapers, including the Baltimore Patriot, which re-titled the poem as "The Star Spangled Banner," better reflecting its content (Lineberry, 2007).

As decades passed, the song remained one of the most popular patriotic songs in America alongside songs such as "Yankee Doodle" or "God Bless America." On March 3, 1931, it was adopted by an act of Congress as the official anthem of the United States of America (History.com editors, 2019).

The "Star Spangled Banner" - a piece of music meant to symbolize the essence of America, was connected to slavery from the beginning: "its author, Francis Scott Key, was a slave owner. Indeed, the oft-overlooked third verse of Key's original text proclaims, "No refuge could save the hireling & slave / From the terror of flight or the gloom of the grave" (Robin, 2016). Abolitionists were always pointing to the incongruence of the American self-proclamation as "the land of the free" while millions of its inhabitants lived in chains. Satirical versions of the "Star Spangled Banner" were common, including this one:

> "Oh, say do you hear, at the dawn's early light," the new version opened. "The shrieks of those bondsmen, whose blood is now streaming. From the merciless lash, while our banner in sight / With its stars, mocking freedom, is fitfully gleaming." The four verses, which are matched carefully to the contours and rhythm of "The Star-Spangled Banner," describe slave ships waving "our star-spangled banner," excoriate "our blood-guilty nation," and conclude with the line "O'er the death-bed of Freedom—the home of the slave." (Robin, 2016).

Although many other political movements satirized the anthem (the temperance movement wrote its own version), the hypocrisy of its lyrics - and America's hypocrisy in general, the land where "all men were created equal" - was always easiest to see in regard to slavery (Robin, 2016). Conflict surrounding the anthem, especially after its adoption in 1931, has been common, especially in times of intense unrest.

America's understanding of its own values can be seen in its history of anthem-related conflict. This conflict is sharpened because, as a piece of music, the anthem resonates profoundly, but differently, with those who hear it. This is in line with all music, as songs can mean different things to different people: music is an inexact form of communication.

The earliest formal test of the anthem came in a pair of Supreme Court cases in the 1940s. These cases illustrate the feedback loop between culture, music, and politics in a clear way, as this particular feedback loop was extraordinarily rapid. Cultural trends often take decades, even centuries, to develop, but in this example, the Supreme Court took the incredibly rare step of reversing its own decision after only three years. In 1940 it ruled that public schools could institute mandatory flag salute rules (and, by extension, could mandate standing for the anthem), but it overturned this decision in 1943. This was not a random decision. The Supreme Court is not fickle - in order to maintain its own legitimacy it rarely, if ever, overturns its past decisions. That is why the outcome of the court case West Virginia State Board of Education v. Barnette is such an extraordinary decision:

> In 1943, at the height of the Second World War, the court heard a challenge by a Jehovah's Witness family to the expulsion of their daughters, Marie and Gathie Barnette, from a school in West Virginia. The sisters had been punished for refusing to salute the flag and repeat the Pledge of Allegiance, something state law required of students. (As Jehovah's Witnesses, the parents did not believe in making such salutes and oaths.) (Toobin, 2016)

Only three years earlier, an almost identical court (only one of the nine justices was different), had ruled in Minersville School District v. Gobiti that "the state's interest in patriotism and 'national cohesion' trumped individual rights, such as freedom of expression." (Scarinci, 2017).

So, what changed in three years? America joined the Second World War, and in doing so developed an extreme distaste for the heightened nationalism of Nazi Germany. The German anthem, along with symbols such as the swastika and the Nazi salute, was used as a loyalty test: conform or die. It was through this lens that the justices rejected the idea that the state should try to enforce patriotism. In the words of the author of the Supreme Court's opinion, "freedom demands that those in power allow others to think for themselves" (Toobin, 2016).

Despite this decision, conflict surrounding the anthem (and the flag) continued. Jimi Hendrix famously played a version of the anthem as a guitar solo meant to protest America's involvement in the Vietnam War, an act considered the "musical equivalent of flag-burning" (Robin, 2016). Actual flag-burning would come before the Supreme Court in 1989 in a case called Texas v. Johnson that was argued along similar lines as both Minersville School District v. Gobiti and West Virginia State Board of Education v. Barnette.

Texas v. Johnson was a landmark Supreme Court decision. The court's vote – a close five to four – declared that burning the flag constituted free speech and was therefore protected under the First Amendment. To oversimplify, the majority found that striking down laws criminalizing flag desecration was unpleasant but necessary. Justice Kennedy succinctly phrased the majority's position that "it is poignant but fundamental that the flag protects those who hold it in contempt" (Texas v. Johnson, 1989).

This decision was extremely unpopular with the public at the time it was made, and remains unpopular to some today. Congress attempted to reverse the Supreme Court's decision, which resulted in the passage of the Flag Protection Act, only to see it struck down by the Supreme Court in United States v. Eichman for the same reasons that Texas v. Johnson was struck down. Following that failure, Congress has periodically attempted to pass a new amendment to enshrine such a law in the Constitution, only to see each attempt fail.

Although all these cases are primarily concerned with the flag, they apply equally to the "Star Spangled Banner," which holds a similar place in America's cultural conscience. There is something intangible to both these symbols, and this history of legislation highlights the complex relationship America has with its own guiding values. The most recent conflict concerning the anthem is ongoing: athletes kneeling.

Kneeling and the Anthem

Although former NFL quarterback Colin Kaepernick (and his teammate Eric Reid) instigated the current anthem conversation, Kaepernick was not the first American athlete to protest during the anthem, nor the first to suffer the consequences. One of the earliest examples of national anthem protests is also one of the most prominent: the 1968 Black Power salute. During the medal ceremony for the 200 meter race, while the national anthem played, the two African American athletes who finished first and third - Tommy Smith and John Carlos respectively - raised their fists in a Black Power salute while standing on the podium (Younge, 2020). Additionally, the white Australian athlete who finished second, Peter Norman, wore an Olympic Project for Human Rights badge (Blakemore, 2018). Their protest started while the anthem played and lasted for its duration.

The reaction was immediate: "as the American athletes raised their fists, the stadium hushed, then burst into racist sneers and angry insults" (Blakemore, 2018). Condemnation from the International Olympic Committee immediately followed, and "the IOC president ordered Smith and Carlos to be suspended from the US team and the Olympic village" (Younge, 2020). U.S. Olympic officials obliged and suspended Smith and Carlos "for politicizing the Games" (David, 2008). Norman was punished by his own country of Australia, which "was experiencing racial tensions of its own. For years, it had been governed by its "White Australia Policy," which dramatically limited immigration to the country by non-white people" (Blakemore, 2018). And although Smith and Carlos were eventually accepted back into America's sports community, Norman "was regularly excluded from events related to the sport. Even when the Olympics came to Sydney in 2000, he was not recognized" (Blakemore, 2018). When he died in 2006, "Carlos and Smith, who had kept in touch with Norman for years, were pallbearers at the Australian's funeral" (Blakemore, 2018). Smith and Carlos raised the Black Power salute during a volatile year in American - and world - history.

> It was 1968; the black power movement had provided a post-civil rights rallying cry and the anti-Vietnam protests were gaining pace ... Martin Luther King had been assassinated and the US had been plunged into yet another year of race riots in its urban centres ... A few weeks before the Games, scores of students and activists had been gunned down by

authorities in Mexico City itself (Younge, 2020).

The backlash was so harsh because, in the midst of this turmoil, the IOC considered the Games to be an apolitical event; it was about sports, not politics. But to Smith and Carlos, this was a joke. Politics had structured their entire experiences, and this had always included sports. In fact, Carlos had originally wanted to be an Olympic swimmer, not a runner, "until his father broke it to him that the training facilities he needed were in private clubs for whites and the wealthy" (Younge, 2020). They chose their protest carefully in order to target the "tropes of American patriotism – flag and anthem" (Younge, 2020).

They were not the first to introduce politics into sports. The original, ancient Olympic games were politicized contests between the city states of Ancient Greece and "during the so-called "Nazi Olympics" of 1936 ... the Olympic torch relay, first introduced that year in Berlin, was meant to provide a symbolic connection between ancient Greece and Rome and Nazi Germany as the center of civilization" (David, 2020). But their example is well-remembered in the American cultural conscience - unlike the example of Mahmoud Abdul-Rauf.

In the 1990s, a decade when athletes often tried to stay as apolitical as possible on the court or field, the NBA player Mahmoud Abdul-Rauf staged his own protest of the anthem by refusing to stand at attention while it played, instead preferring to stretch or remain in the locker room (Washington, 2016). "Like Kaepernick, Abdul-Rauf said he viewed the American flag as a symbol of oppression and racism. Abdul-Rauf also said standing for the anthem would conflict with his Muslim faith." (Washington, 2016).

The backlash was strong, highlighting how important this music was to so many people. Despite being the leading scorer on his team, Abdul-Rauf was traded at the season's end and found himself out of the NBA at the young age of 29 (Washington, 2016). He faced death threats and his property was vandalized by spray paint spelling out 'KKK' (Washington, 2016). His principled stand likely cost him tens of millions of dollars in lost salary. Abdul-Rauf captured the crux of the conflict in this quote: "It's not representing what you say it's representing. So as far as I'm concerned, I can't honor this symbol that doesn't represent those values"" (Fedotin, 2018).

The same debate bubbled up two decades later when Colin Kaepernick decided to protest the treatment of African Americans in the United States by kneeling as the anthem played. Many criticized him on the grounds that kneeling during the anthem was disrespectful toward the men and women of the military, whom those people most associated with the anthem. Others defended his right to kneel as the very embodiment of the freedom the anthem represented. As Abdul-Rauf said, both sides did not think the anthem represented what the other side said the anthem represented.

What this communicates to us is not just that two different groups cannot agree on the meaning of a song. The anthem supposedly represents the essence of America, therefore, these two groups are disagreeing about what that essence is. The power of music - to convey moods and emotions otherwise impossible to communicate - is also its weakness, as the interpretation of music is an individual act. And in the anthem's case, the interpretation of music is the interpretation of an entire nation's values. Any individual or group of individuals that does not think America is living up to its values might feel part of the solidarity the anthem is supposed to engender. Instead, they might look to another musical source that captures their mood and communicates their values. This is especially clear in the conjoined traditions of African American music and African American politics.

CHAPTER 16: WE SHALL OVERCOME

The lyrics to "We Shall Overcome" consist mainly of the titular phrase being repeated. "We shall overcome / we shall overcome / we shall overcome ..." chanted slowly, like a hymn or an anthem. As far as music goes, it is extraordinarily simple, which makes the reason it was adopted by the Civil Rights movement easy to understand: the movement felt it needed to overcome the unjust political structures of America. This could not be done by adopting America's anthem, which rang false to oppressed ears, and so another had to be chosen. The simplicity of "We Shall Overcome" was not the only reason it was chosen. If the core of the Civil Rights movement - the African American community - felt that "We Shall Overcome" expressed their experience of America better than "The Star Spangled Banner," we can examine American history to find out why.

THE ANTEBELLUM SOUTH AND EMANCIPATION

The Antebellum South refers to the American South during the three decades preceding the Civil War (antebellum is Latin for "before (the) war") (PBS, n.d.). During this time, slavery was legal in America. Music was integral to the enslaved people of America. For one, it fulfilled music's most basic purpose: to communicate; "slaves from different countries, tribes, and cultures used singing as a way to communicate ... They were able to look for kin, countrymen and women through song" (Berry, 2017). This was especially vital because "slaves' lives were restricted in innumerable ways, but among them included limits on literacy"

(Smithsonian, n.d.). With other forms of communication limited, extra importance was placed upon music. And music is more than a source of communication - it is a source of joy, a source of expression, a catharsis through which we express pain and sorrow: "music was a way for slaves to express their feelings whether it was sorrow, joy, inspiration or hope. Songs were passed down from generation to generation throughout slavery" (Berry, 2017).

The earliest forms of "We Shall Overcome" were sung by slaves during this period: "'We Shall Overcome' began as a folk song, a work song. Slaves in the fields would sing, 'I'll be all right someday.' It became known in the churches" (Adams, 2013). Once the enslaved were emancipated, the church became the dominant social structure of the African American community, as it "was the first social institution fully controlled by black men in America, and its multiple functions testified to its centrality in the black community (Foner, 2014, p. 92).

The "Star Spangled Banner" did enjoy a brief spike of popularity among the freedmen after the war: the mood of those freed was jubilant. The emotional reaction of the formerly enslaved upon emancipation was painted by the incredibly talented pen of W.E.B. Du Bois: "All that was Beauty, all that was Love, all that was Truth, stood on the top of these mad mornings and sang with the stars. A great human sob shrieked in the wind, and tossed its tears upon the sea,—free, free, free" (Du Bois, 1935). Of course, the so-called "freedom" promised by the Constitution and sang about in the anthem was denied to the freedmen. This was not a Southern response: it was an American one. New York City, the heart of the North, experienced a draft riot in 1863 that "degenerated into a virtual racial pogrom, with uncounted numbers of blacks murdered on the streets or driven to take refuge in Central Park or across the river in New Jersey" (Foner, 2014, p. 32). During that time:

> A child of 3 years of age was thrown from a 4th story window and instantly killed. A woman one hour after her confinement was set upon and beaten with her tender babe in her arms....Children were torn from their mother's embrace and their brains blown out in the very face of the afflicted mother. Men were burnt by slow fires (Foner, 2014, p. 33).

The African American struggle to overcome was just beginning.

THE CIVIL RIGHTS MOVEMENT

The next century of American history was a reign of terror for African Americans: "someone was lynched, on average, every four days from 1889 to 1929" (Kendi, 2016, p. 259). The "land of the free" was certainly the "home of the brave," yet most of the brave inhabitants sang hymns instead of the anthem of their oppressors. Yet, the 1950s brought hope for positive change, and the tenor of "We Shall Overcome" changed from mournful, with its sights set on the afterlife, to defiant, with its sights set on equality.

Many mark the 1954 Brown v. Board of Education Supreme Court decision as the "beginning of the black freedom movement of the 1950s and 1960s" (Cone, 1991, p. 8). This 1954 decision, while momentous, only professed equality on paper. The result of the decision was that race-based segregation at public school was declared illegal, which was a blow to segregation in general; but, it was up to the states to enforce this decision. Emmett Till, a 14 year old African American boy, was lynched that same year, revealing "a gaping chasm between real life and the Supreme Court's arid pronouncement of equality in law" (Branch, 2013, p. 6). A few years later in 1963, four young African American girls were murdered when their church in Birmingham was bombed, which itself was only a few months after the Civil Rights leader Medgar Evers was shot dead on his doorstep in front of his family. It was in response to this that Martin Luther King Jr. proclaimed that "we must be concerned not merely about who murdered them, but about the system, the way of life and the philosophy which produced the murderers" (Cone, 1991, p. 85).

At this point, the Civil Rights activists were not singing the "Star Spangled Banner," as the anthem represented the very system King was denouncing. America was divided, and this division could be represented in music: those opposing the Civil Rights activists often did so while waving the American flag and proudly echoing the anthem, while the activists sang "We Shall Overcome" in response. Legendary Civil Rights leader John Lewis recalled how "'We Shall Overcome' sustained him throughout the years of struggle — especially those moments when demonstrators who had been beaten, arrested, or detained would stand and sing it together" (Adams, 2013). This was not an easy task more often than not. John Lewis was a Freedom Rider. Freedom Riders were a multiracial group who challenged the government to uphold the law pertaining to buses being desegregated. They would ride the buses into the Deep South. They were often attacked, such as when "on Sunday, May 14, 1961, a white mob attacked and burned one bus of Freedom Riders outside Anniston, Alabama. Minutes later, a Ku Klux Klan posse severely beat the second busload on arrival at the Trailways station in Birmingham" (Branch, 2013, p. 24). In the "land of the free," "63 percent of all Americans disapproved of the Freedom Rides" (Branch, 2013, p. 38). America did not want the Civil Rights activists to "overcome."

Yet "We Shall Overcome" helped create real, lasting impact. Through music, the Civil Rights activists were able to affect the political structures of America. One of the most infamous moments of the Civil Rights Movement was "Bloody Sunday," a day when a group of marchers led by John Lewis were beaten by cattle prods and mauled by dogs on national television while singing "We Shall Overcome" (Cone, 1991, p. 216). President Lyndon B. Johnson immediately demanded that Congress pass the Voting Rights act that the activists had been marching for. This act would make it easier for African Americans to vote by removing any restrictions that prevented them from voting. President Johnson gave a speech before Congress that included these lines: "Their cause must be our cause, too, because it's not just Negroes, but really, it's all of us who must overcome the crippling legacy of bigotry and injustice. And we shall overcome" (Adams, 2013). "We Shall Overcome" had reached the uppermost echelon of American power, and the Voting Rights Act of 1965 was passed soon after.

CHAPTER 17: HAMILTON

HAMILTON

Music and politics intersect in many places. The discussion so far has been centred around songs sung in solidarity - anthem-like songs like the "Star Spangled Banner" or "We Shall Overcome." These songs, along with hymns, are most often musically simple, with lyrics designed to be sung in a group. But music has many, many genres, and all of them have political potential.

America's musical and political traditions have developed in the context of America's developing culture. The anthem was composed as a contemporary song; that is, its particular style fit into the popular music of the time. Although the hymnal style is no longer popular outside of churches, all genres of music that became popular throughout American history have all had political uses. These uses can be overt, for example if the lyrics are explicitly political, or they can be subtle; if the genre is associated with a particular cultural milieu, such as rock and roll and the counterculture movement or hip hop and the African American community.

Genres such as hip hop that have political associations have plenty of overtly political songs. This was true during the counterculture movement, with songs such as "Mississippi Goddamn" by Nina Simone or most of Bob Dylan's discography. And it is true of hip hop, which has a rich history of political music. Many of the most popular songs in the history of hip hop are blatantly political, such as "Fight the Power" by Public Enemy or "Fuck tha Police" by N.W.A. (Kendi, 2016, p. 443).

It was for both these subtle and overt reasons that Lin-Manuel Miranda chose to use hip hop to tell the story of Alexander Hamilton, one of America's Founding Fathers, in the form of a Broadway play. The play, "Hamilton," set Broadway ticket sale records (Viagas, 2015). It was critically acclaimed, scoring "a record-setting 16 Tony Award nominations" (Chow, 2020). "Hamilton" blends music, politics, and culture together into "an opulent, richly layered meta-text about the impossibility of fully accurate historical storytelling, about the American dream, and implicitly about the people of color who are so often left out of the narrative of that dream" (Romano, 2020). But, in order to properly examine the relationship between music and politics present in "Hamilton," a quick introduction to the history of political hip hop is needed to contextualize the importance of its role in the play.

A Brief History of Political Hip Hop

The earliest hip-hop and rap music can be traced to the African American community of 1970's New York City (Dixon, 2015). Like the appropriately named genre of country music, hip hop grew out of its environment: "hip-hop music began to develop as a local underground art form, with lyrics that spoke out on urban poverty, racism, and a growing sense of economic abandonment in African-American inner city neighborhoods" (Dixon, 2015). It was performed at events, on the street, at parties, and part of a larger culture that included DJs, breakdancing, and graffiti artists. It grew more complex in the 1980s and spread across America. This evolution was called New School Hip-Hop, and by the late 1980s, it was far closer in form to today's hip-hop than it had been just a half-decade before.

The hip hop community made music that expressed their lived experience, and since many believed their lived experience was heavily influenced by political oppression, the songs were inherently political in nature. This early history of hip hop meant that even as the years passed, the genre would always be connected to its founding figures - and therefore to politics. The Golden Age of Hip-Hop, from the late 1980s to the mid 1990s, was characterized by its political flavour, especially in comparison to the other popular genres.

Because hip hop is most strongly associated with African Americans, its political nature is linked to the concerns of African Americans. The aforementioned song "Fuck tha Police" enjoyed a revival in popularity in the aftermath of the Rodney King beating in 1992 (Kendi, 2016, p. 447). More recently, songs such as "walking in the snow" by the rap duo Run the Jewels speak out against ongoing police brutality with lyrics like: "And every day on the evening news, they feed you fear for free / And you so numb, you watch the cops choke out a man like me /

Until my voice goes from a shriek to whisper, "I can't breathe." Although the song was released in the immediate aftermath of George Floyd's death, the lyrics were written beforehand and were inspired by the death of Eric Garner - another African American man suffocated by a police officer. These songs are not usually chanted in large groups in the way that "We Shall Overcome" or the "Star Spangled Banner," but they still serve to bring people together by allowing them to express emotions in a way that only music can.

But a (morbidly) fascinating chapter of hip-hop's history is the geographic rivalries that dominated the 1990s - rivalries that resulted in murder and mayhem. This underscores the cultural importance of the genre - it was more than music: it was distilled cultural expression. The leading voices of the two main geographic factions of this rivalry were The Notorious B.I.G. and Tupac Shakur of the East coast and West coast respectively. As hip-hop spread across the country, it came to reflect the specific areas it was in. These areas then grew protective of their art, proclaiming it as their genre. Rappers on both coasts would write and release songs insulting the other coast, and the war of words grew into a war with real, physical consequences. Both the Notorious B.I.G. and Tupac Shakur were killed, resulting in the gradual dissipation of the rivalry over the next few years. In the decades since, hip-hop has gained cultural prominence and diversified into many different subgenres such as crunk, alternative, trap, mumble, and more. But "Hamilton" was the first notable example of hip-hop's introduction to the world of musical theatre.

The Genius of Hamilton

The music of "Hamilton" is integral to its genius - it is a musical, after all - but the genius of "Hamilton" is holistic. The play strikes at the heart of the American essence: the Founding Fathers, who are the predominant figures of America's founding mythology. This mythology is somewhat unique in modern countries, perhaps comparable to the legend of Romulus and Remus in ancient Rome. Most other modern countries do not revere their founding figures nearly as strongly as the Americans revere theirs. The American Founding Fathers are still very important in contemporary American culture, and their names are invoked to lend weight to particular causes. Their legacy is constantly re-evaluated, often in ways that support the evaluator's ideology.

Such scrutiny is made possible by the abundance of primary sources available. Although the Constitution is the most famous, we can read their personal correspondence, works of literature (such as "The Rights of Man" by Thomas Paine), political tracts (such as the Federalist Papers), and more. Additionally, many of their contemporaries wrote about them and the events they were involved in. Newspapers, diaries, letters: thousands have survived, allowing us to reconstruct their lives with remarkable amounts of details. And sometimes reconstruction is not even necessary, for we can visit their literal homes, such as the forced labour camp (called a plantation) Monticello owned by Thomas Jefferson, which you can tour today if you wish.

Altogether, this goes to say that the Founding Fathers are symbols, much like the flag or the anthem. Their virtues and vices are often emphasized based upon contemporary morals or trends. This can be done through the work of historians, through political movements, through cultural moments, or through art. "Hamilton" is an excellent example of this.

Lin Manuel-Miranda, the playwright of "Hamilton," wanted to present his own version of the Founding Fathers. The resulting play reflects contemporary American ideology in a brilliant and accessible manner. Through a diverse cast and the use of hip-hop, Miranda presented these symbols of America - the Founding Fathers - so that they matched what America is today. According to Miranda, he chose a racially diverse cast because ""this is what our country looks like, and the audience accepts it," says Miranda. "In so many ways, the people we call the Founding Fathers are these mythic figures – but they were people. I think the casting of the show humanizes them, in a way, because they're not these distant marble creatures" (Vozick-Levinson, 2015).

Although it is true that casting the Founding Fathers - who were all white men - as people of colour humanizes them to a contemporary audience, Miranda's choice is primarily a symbolic one. Everyone knows the Foundings Fathers were white men, but that is not the point. If they represent the essence of America, then his casting choice chooses to treat the Founding Fathers as symbols rather than purely historical figures. He is claiming these symbols for contemporary America - for a diverse America.

The effect of the diverse casting is heightened by the choice of hip-hop for all the play's music. As we explored previously, hip-hop has a strong connection to the culture and politics of the African American community. This was not a community with members present among the Founding Fathers (except as the property of some). The addition of hip-hop imbues the setting with a contemporary tone that the casting alone does not. Additionally, there is a practical aspect to the inclusion of hip-hop: it is a relatively accommodating form of music for storytelling. The structure of the lyrical composition translates well to the musical form, which is utilized by Miranda throughout the play in character conversations and debates.

Together, the music and the casting work together to make "Hamilton" a smashing success. Many people walked away feeling more connected to America, more invested in a nation that represented them and their values, and more included in their nation's history. As Daveed Diggs, the actor who plays Thomas Jefferson, said: "'I walked out of the show with a sense of ownership over American history. Part of it is seeing brown bodies play these people" (Monteiro, 2016, p. 93).

The choice of hip-hop undoubtedly boosted the astounding popularity of "Hamilton." It also helped many American's feel a "sense of ownership" over their history by communicating it to them via a method they were familiar with and appreciated. One of the virtues of music mentioned often in this book is its ability to bring people together. "Hamilton" brought a truly diverse group of Americans together through song and story.

Criticism of Hamilton

"Hamilton" is a work of historical fiction: it uses people who really existed in a certain historical period to tell a story. Because this period of history - the American Revolution and its aftermath - is so vital to the ideals of contemporary America, it is impossible for "Hamilton" to be politically neutral. In a true "damned if you do, damned if you don't" scenario: even an attempt at political neutrality regarding the Founding Fathers is a political act.

"Hamilton" does not shy away from its status as a work of political art, nor does it pretend it does not interpret history. One of the reasons Miranda wrote the play is for students. As Miranda said, "this [is a] very dense, historically accurate musical [that] makes these people [the Founding Fathers] come alive in their [the students'] heads" (Vozick-Levinson, 2015). Although musical theatre is as valid a form of communicating history as any other, there are certain risks involved. Consider this quote from an article reviewing "Hamilton": "knowing the real history allows one to fully appreciate the artistry involved in condensing material and making necessary alterations to keep the story moving forward smoothly" (Gordon-Reed, 2016). If someone watches "Hamilton" and bases their knowledge of history off of it, they will be basing it off a condensed and altered version of that history. That is not always a bad thing, but when historical interpretations of the Founding Fathers often determine entire political ideologies and guide contemporary political arguments, any alteration matters.

History shows that historical fiction can have a profound influence on a society. American history is replete with examples, such as Uncle Tom's Cabin, whose author Abraham Lincoln allegedly called "that little woman who started this big war," (Largent, n.d.) or To Kill a Mockingbird, which American's consistently rank as one of the books that most affected their life. But the most extreme example of a work of historical fiction that had the most direct impact on America was the 1915 film "Birth of a Nation." "In just over three hours, D.W. Griffith's controversial epic film about the Civil War and Reconstruction depicted the Ku Klux Klan as valiant saviors of a post-war South ravaged by Northern carpetbaggers and immoral freed blacks" (Clark, 2019). The film was critically lauded, screened at the White House, and was (and still is) used by the Ku Klux

Klan as a recruiting tool (Clark, 2019). Its membership exploded. Not only that, the film (along with Gone with the Wind), helped make the Stars and Bars Confederate flag popular; formerly, it was the little-known battle flag for the Army of Northern Virginia (Chapman, 2011, p. 114).

Of course, "Hamilton" is very different than "Birth of a Nation." The point is that highly innovative forms of art used to tell historical fiction set in politically fraught periods of history can make an impact. The question is: how responsible are the creators of that art for its accuracy, its impact, and its message?

Just as "Hamilton" makes certain presentation choices in regards to its casting and its music, it makes narrative choices. For many, the most controversial decision Lin Manuel Miranda made concerns both: the decision to cast people of colour in the roles of white historical figures such as George Washington and Thomas Jefferson, which can be seen as "a somewhat audacious choice given that both men are strongly associated with owning, and in the case of the latter, raping and impregnating slaves" (Nichols, 2016). As Romano notes: "the problem with this is twofold: it sanitizes the crimes of enslavers and it erases real people from the narrative because "the show has zero named characters of color" (2020).

Supporters of "Hamilton" often applaud it for writing nonwhite people into history (perhaps even mythology) of America's founding. But some people argue that: "you don't actually need to 'write nonwhite people into the story.' As historians have pointed out, there were plenty of nonwhite people around at the time, people who already had fully-developed stories and identities. But none of these people appears in the play" (Nichols, 2016). As the historian Lyra Monteiro points out, "in the 1790s, a slave was present in one in five of the city's white households. Thus, every scene in the play contains an opportunity for an enslaved character—from the tavern where the revolutionaries meet in act 1, to the Winter's Ball where Hamilton meets his future wife, Eliza" (2016, p. 94). And the famous African American playwright Ishmael Reed raised a particularly disturbing point in his scathing critique of the play: "Can you imagine Jewish actors in Berlin's theaters taking roles of Goering? Goebbels? Eichmann? Hitler?" (Reed, 2015).

The point is that "with a cast dominated by actors of color, the play is nonetheless yet another rendition of the "exclusive past," with its focus on the deeds of "great white men" and its silencing of the presence and contributions of people of color in the Revolutionary era" (Monteiro, 2016, p. 90). To its critics, "Hamilton" is a form of double erasure because its casting and narrative choices suggest that only these "great white men" represent the founding ideals of America and only by reimagining their story can we reimagine America. But what if we reimagined America by telling the stories of the marginalised and the oppressed?

Another narrative alteration is Alexander Hamilton's character. The titular character is presented far more sympathetically than history suggests him to be. He "simply didn't believe in democracy, which he labeled an American "disease." He fought—with military force—any model of organizing the American political economy that might promote egalitarian politics. He was an authoritarian, and proud of it" (Stoller, 2017). The play makes him out to be an abolitionist when in reality, he profited from enslaved labour, may have enslaved fellow humans at some point, and married into one of the richest slave-owning families in New York (Monteiro, 2016, p. 98). And his attitude (and policy history) regarding America's indigenous population was genocidal: "[in] a letter Hamilton wrote in 1791 … he cheerfully described the imminent attack of Kentucky settlers on a Native American community: "Corps of ardent Volunteers on their route to demolish every savage man, woman and Child."" (Chow, 2020).

Critics of "Hamilton" believe these narrative choices matter because they know that most people will not go beyond the songs for their historical education. Music has incredible communicative powers, but those powers often benefit mood and emotion over detailed historical accuracy. The jubilant, braggadocious opening lines of "Hamilton" ("working a lot harder / by being a lot smarter, / by being a self-starter") are not as fun when you realize Alexander Hamilton did not work harder than the enslaved, he was not smarter than the enslaved, and he was not more of a self-starter than the enslaved. Rather, he was white.

Conclusion

We have examined several manifestations of the relationship between music and politics. They each trace their roots to collective identity, and from these shared roots springs their relationship. At its best, music can inspire political movements that bring people together. It can allow people from all backgrounds to feel a sense of solidarity and it can express our deepest cultural identities. It can supplement other forms of political art and it can allow communication across partisan divides that words can't breach. Music, implicitly or explicitly, always has the chance to be a political act.

CONCLUSION

As we have well established by this point, music is a large and complicated entity, which can be understood and considered from a wide variety of disciplines. It is with us every step of our journey through life, and as we learned, impacts every step we make in subtle, yet important ways. This book allowed us to consider music through the lens of five disciplines: science, linguistics, communication, philosophy, and politics, and doing so allowed us to broaden our horizons and truly take the time to consider the music we listen to, why we listen to it, why we enjoy it, and what it is trying to tell us.

We began by perusing through a brief history of western art music so that we had enough background in the history of what most of us consider to be 'classical' music to understand which musical forms fit where in history, as well as a basic understanding of the evolution of music itself as a form. This allowed us to then discuss some important musical forms, which we talked about throughout the text. Understanding the history of the form, as well as general expectations for the form, helped us go into further detail in our analyses of compositions that use each of the forms.

Our first section discussed the science of music, through the lens of physics, chemistry, biology, and psychology. In the physics section, we learned about the basis of sound: how it is created, how it is disseminated, and how it changes depending on a variety of circumstances. This information allowed us to move forward to the chemistry section, where we learned about specific ways in which music impacts our brain chemistry, and how our body is impacted by the chemicals our brain releases when we listen to specific songs. From there, we delved into the biology of the ear, so we could understand exactly how sound travels from the air into our brain. Finally, we discussed psychology: the psychology of music and emotion, of music and memory, of music therapy, and of music and identity. Within this section, we learned that music can be beneficial to individuals with brain trauma or disease, that we engage with the emotion in a song through emotional mimicry, and the ways in which music plays into our intrinsic and extrinsic identities. Our second section looked at linguistics, and attempted to answer the question: is music truly a language? After discussing the building blocks that make up a language, we established that music doesn't constitute a language in a linguistic sense, but that it still has many aspects that are similar to that of a language. This discussion allowed us to move into a brief history of musical notation, or music as a written language, which then also allowed us to move into a new question: how does language affect music? The case study we considered demonstrated the effectiveness of utilizing happy music with sad lyrics, which is just one reason analyzing both is extremely important.

In the communications section, we began by considering the difference between music and form, and how musical form makes up the basis of our musical expectations. After delving into musical expectations and how musical signposting helps listeners feel as if they have some kind of control over where the music is going, we jumped right into the theory of semiotics, and learned about how to apply semiotics in our everyday lives. This led us into musical semiotics, where we established how to take the signs we had talked out in our everyday lives and find them in the music we listen to. We learned about three types of signs, which we then went on to analyze in our three case studies. Schubert's Erlkönig taught us about the importance of key and lyrical tone, the fifth movement of Berlioz's Symphonie Fantastique taught us that innovation and instrumentation are two key methods of creating discomfort in listeners, and the Beatles' "Paperback Writer" taught us about the importance of word choice within a song, as well as the effects of innovation of recording technology. These case studies then allowed us to move forth in semiotic analysis of the music we listen to on a daily basis.

Our philosophy section took us through a fascinating and vivid exploration of philosophical thought regarding music through the ages. We explored the ways in which the ancients, medievals, moderns, and 20th century philosophers considered music, how that differed between philosophers within the same age, and how it changed depending on the era. From Plato and Aristotle to Adorno and Scruton, we considered what makes music beautiful, how we should enjoy music in order for it to be beautiful, and what aspects of music truly speak to us as individuals. By understanding the philosophical thought surrounding music, we are then able to take a deeper and more thorough gander through the music in our own lives, thinking about what that music truly means to us and how it speaks to our philosophical side.

Finally, we explored the connection between music and politics, considering the American national anthem, "We Shall Overcome," and songs from the Broadway musical Hamilton. Our discussion of the American national anthem discussed the ways in which the national anthem serves the American people, and how it has been criticised for only serving some of the American people. We discussed the Civil Rights movement, and the ways in which music - particularly "We Shall Overcome" - provided hope and togetherness to those who struggled to see the light at the end of the tunnel. Finally, we analyzed Lin Manuel Miranda's hit Broadway show Hamilton, and considered some of the ways in which its portrayals of American history through song impacted the way in which we understand the political aspects of history as it happened.

Throughout all of our discussions, one thing has been inevitably clear: music plays a huge part in all of our lives in more ways than we could ever imagine. Our goal, with this book, was to demonstrate just some of the many ways that we can create deeper connections with the music we listen to, and be able to dissect and identify some of the ways in which the music is intended to connect to us. Now, we invite you to go forth into the musical world of your choosing, but to do so with an open mind. Think about the way the music is created. Think about how that impacts your body and mind. Think about the way in which the music is written: is it a language? Consider some of the semiotic ways in which the composer is trying to speak directly to you: to make you feel something you've never felt before. Analyze the music using some philosophical thought and logic. Consider the potential political implications of the music you listen to. There are many ways for you to understand and interact with music, and we are happy to have given you the tools with which to do so.

GLOSSARY OF TERMS

INTRODUCTION

Aria: "an extended piece for solo singer that has much more musical elaboration and coherence than a passage of recitative. The vocal part is more melodic, the rhythm is more consistent, the meter clearer, and typically the accompaniment includes the entire orchestra" (Kerman & Tomlinson, 2015, p. 84).

Cadenza: "unaccompanied bravura passage introduced at or near the close of a movement of a composition and serving as a brilliant climax, particularly in the solo concerti of a virtuoso character" (Encyclopaedia Britannica, 2020).

Character Piece: Short compositions whose fundamental purpose is to describe a certain character, be it a person, an emotion, an object, or something else entirely. As Kerman & Tomlinson note: "each [character piece] conveys an intense, distinct emotion - an emotion often hinted at by an imaginative title supplied by the composer (2015, p. 243).

Concerto: "a large composition for orchestra and solo instrument (Kerman & Tomlinson, 2015, p. 424).

Consonance: "the impression of stability and repose... experienced by a listener when certain combinations of tones or notes are sounded together" (Encyclopaedia Britannica, 2020).

Development: Second of three sections in sonata form. Takes all of the themes and keys in the exposition and breaks them down so that they can be built up in new ways: "That is, themes or fragments of themes may appear in new keys; they may be combined to form apparently new melodies; they may be played against each other as counterpoint, or countermelody" (Encyclopaedia Britannica, 2020).

Dissonance: the impression of tension or clash ... experienced by a listener when certain combinations of tones or notes are sounded together" (Encyclopaedia Britannica, 2020).

Exposition: First of three sections in sonata form. "A large, diverse section of music in which the basic material of the movement is presented" (Kerman & Tomlinson, 2015, p. 163).

Expressionism: Music characterized by high levels of dissonance, distorted melodies and harmonies, and lots of dynamic contrast, and "exploited extreme states, extending all the way to hysteria, nightmare, even insanity" (Kerman & Tomlinson, 2015, p. 320).

Fugue: A typical Baroque musical form which "uses only one theme throughout - like a single extended point of imitation - and often treats that theme with great contrapuntal ingenuity and learning" (Kerman & Tomlinson, 2015, p. 91).

Homophony: "music in a harmonic, chordal texture" (Kerman & Tomlinson, 2015, p. 61).

Impressionism: A musical style that was a reaction against the rhetoric of romanticism, disrupting the forward motion of standard harmonic progressions" (Encyclopaedia Britannica, 2020) Debussy's Clouds is one popular example of impressionistic music.

Movement: "self-contained section of music that is part of a larger work" (Kerman & Tomlinson, 2015, p. 116).
Music: "a pattern of sounds made by musical instruments, voices, or computers, or a combination of these, intended to give pleasure to people listening to it" (Cambridge Dictionary, 2020).

Organum: "consisted of two melodic lines moving simultaneously note against note" (Encyclopaedia Britannica, 2020).

Polyphony: "the simultaneous combination of two or more melodies" (Kerman & Tomlinson, 2015, p. 52).

Program Music: "a term for instrumental music written in association with a poem, a story, or some literary source - or even just a highly suggestive word or two" (Kerman & Tomlinson, 2015, p. 228). "Instrumental music that carries some extramusical meaning, some 'program' of literary idea, legend, scenic description, or personal drama" (Encyclopaedia Britannica, 2020).

Recapitulation: Third of three sections in sonata form. Repeats the exposition section with minor changes; notably, the exposition is played solely in the second key, not the original key.

Ritornello form: "characterised by a recurring A section in between new sections of music, and is often described as 'ABACA', where the A section contains a distinctive theme. Importantly, the recurring A section is rarely an identical repeat of the first time we hear it" (MyTutor, 2019).

Scherzo: In rapid 3/4 time was replete with elements of surprise in dynamics and orchestration" (Encyclopaedia Britannica, 2020).

Sonata Form: Often the form of the opening movement in a symphony with three basic elements: "exposition, development, and recapitulation, in which the musical subject matter is stated, explored or expanded, and restated" (Encyclopaedia Britannica, 2020).

String Quartet: "an ensemble of four solo strings, traditionally two violins, viola, and cello. Through achievements of Haydn, Mozart, and Beethoven, it has come to symbolise the loftiest form of discourse in instrumental music" (BBC Music Magazine, 2016).

Strophic: Repeating the music for each new stanza of the poem" (Encyclopaedia Britannica, 2020).
Troubadours: "one of a class of lyric poets and poet-musicians often of nightly rank who flourished from the 11th to the end of the 13th century, chiefly in the south of France and the north of Italy, and whose major theme was courtly love" (Merriam-Webster, 2020).

Variation Form: "a form in which a single melodic unit is repeated with harmonic, rhythmic, dynamic, or timbral changes" (Kerman & Tomlinson, 2015, p. 430). One of the defining features of variation form is repetition, like ritornello form, but it's often the repetition of a strong bass line, often called the basso ostinato.

Section 1:

Destructive Interference: In music, destructive interference causes silence because "when two opposite waveforms are added, they cancel out, leaving silence" (Hollis, 2017).

Emotion: "a complex experience of consciousness, bodily sensation, and behaviour that reflects the personal significance of a thing, an event, or a state of affairs" (Encyclopedia Britannica, 2020).

Emotional Mimicry: mimicking emotions experienced around us.

Frequency: "the number of cycles per second that passes by a given location" (440). Frequency is measured in hertz. An excellent way to understand frequency is to use one of Young and Stadler's examples: the different sounds that occur when you press different numbers while dialing a phone number. Each number sounds different because it occurs on a different frequency, with some smaller waves having a higher number of cycles per second, and some larger waves having a lower number of cycles per second (Young & Stadler, 2018, p. 440-441).

Musical Tone: "sound that can be recognized by its regularity of vibration" (Encyclopedia Britannica, 2020)

Neurotransmitters: A type of chemical messenger that sends signals by way of synaptic transmission.They have an essential function in the way in which one neuron or neural cell communicates with another and therefore vital for our brains to function.

Nodes: "positions on a standing wave where the wave stays in a fixed position overtime because of destructive interference" (Khan Academy, 2020).

Overtones: "The other frequencies besides the fundamental that exist in musical instruments. Instruments of different shapes and actions produce different overtones. The overtones combine to form the characteristic sound of the instrument" (Hollis, 2017).

Pitch: In music, [the] position of a single sound in the complete range of sound. Sounds are higher or lower in pitch according to the frequency of vibration of the sound waves producing them. A high frequency (e.g., 880 Hz) is perceived as high pitch and a low frequency (e.g., 55 Hz) as a low pitch (Encyclopedia Britannica, 2020).

Psychology: "a scientific discipline that studies mental states and processes and behaviour in humans and other animals" (Encyclopedia Britannica, 2020).

Sound: "a longitudinal wave that is created by a vibrating object, such as a guitar string, the human vocal cords, or the diaphragm of a loudspeaker. Moreover, sound can be created or transmitted only in a medium, such as a gas, liquid, or solid" (Young & Stadler, 2018, p. 439).

Sound Intensity: "the sound power (P) that passes perpendicularly through a surface divided by the area (A) of that surface" (Young & Stadler, 2018, p. 446); the equation for which would resemble $I = PA$ where I is the sound intensity, P is the sound power, and A is the surface area.

Standing Wave: "waves which appear to be oscillating vertically without travelling horizontally. [Standing waves are] created from waves with identical frequency and amplitude interfering with one another while travelling in opposite directions" (Khan Academy, 2020).

Threshold for Hearing: "the smallest sound intensity that the human ear can detect" (Young & Stadler, 2018, p. 447)

Section 2:

Language: Human language is a system. In other words, it is highly structured and operates according to a set of principles. Every language is governed by rules for the formation of words and sentences; these rules constitute its grammar. In order for us to learn a language, the set of rules must be finite in number, but with these rules we can produce an infinite number of sentences and understand sentences which we have never heard before. Theoretically, we could also produce sentences of infinite length, though there are practical limits imposed by memory and the physiology of speech. It is for these reasons that we say human language is infinite or creative (L. J. Brinton & L. K. Arnovick, 2017, p.3).

Morphology: "study of the form and formation of words in a particular language" (Brinton and Arnovick, p.4).

Music: "sound organized in time, intended for, or perceived as, aesthetic experience' (Rodriguez, 1995, cited in Dowling, 2001:470).

Musical Notation: "a visual record of heard or imagined musical sound, or a set of visual instructions for performance of music. It usually takes written or printed form and is a conscious, comparatively laborious process" (brittanica.com, 2020).

Neumes: "any of various symbols representing from one to four notes, used in the musical notation of the Middle Ages but now employed solely in the notation of Gregorian chant in the liturgical books of the Roman Catholic Church" (Dictionary.com).

Phonology: "the study of the sound system of a particular language, the distinctive speech sounds, the combination of sounds that are possible, and features such as intonation and stress" (Brinton and Arnovick, 2017, p.4).

Syntax: "the study of how words are arranged into higher units, such as phrases, clauses, and sentences" (Brinton and Arnovick, pp.4-5).

Universal: "a feature that appears in every musical system" (Patel, 2007, pp. 11-12).

Section 3:

Bridge: Connects two parts of a song, letting listeners know that they are near the end of a song , but that there is still one chorus left before the end.

Cognitive Dissonance: "the distressing mental state caused by inconsistency between a person's two beliefs or a belief and an action" (Griffin et al., 2015, p. 200).

Dynamics: "the volume of sound; the loudness or softness of a musical passage" (Kerman & Tomlinson, 2015, p. 424).

Iconic Sign: "have a perceived resemblance with the objects they portray. They look, sound, taste, smell, or feel similar to their referents" (Griffin et al., 2015, p. 336).

Indexical Sign: "are directly connected with their referents spatially, temporally, or by cause and effect. Like an index finger, they point to the object, action, or idea to which they refer" (Griffin et al., 2015, p. 336).

Idee Fixe: "an obsession; the term used by Berlioz for a recurring theme used in all the movements of one of his program symphonies" (2015, p. 425).

Key: "the major or minor scale around which a piece of music revolves. A song in a major key is based on a major scale. A song in a minor key is based on a minor scale" (Pouska, 2020).

Music: "a pattern of sounds made by musical instruments, voices, or computers, or a combination of these, intended to give pleasure to people listening to it" (Cambridge Dictionary, 2020).

Musical Form: "the structure of a musical composition" (Encyclopaedia Britannica, 2020).

Musical Expectation: The idea that once you have a certain amount of musical knowledge, you are able to subconsciously anticipate what should be coming next.

Musical Signpost: It's the composer's way of telling us where we are in a musical piece, and where we are on our way to. Most of these musical signposts are built into specific musical forms, but on occasion and particularly when composers are breaking away from pre-existing musical forms, they will utilize musical signposts to help ease the transition where they feel necessary.

Semiotics: "the study of the social production of meaning from sign systems; the analysis of anything that can stand for anything else"

(Griffin et al., 2015, p. 327).

Sign: "the inseparable combination of the signifier and the signified" (Griffin et al., 2015, p. 328). The signifier, then, is "the physical form of the sign as we perceive it through our senses; an image" and the signified is "the meaning we associate with the sign" (Griffin et al., 2015, p. 328).

Signpost: Direct us to the places we are going, while also reminding us of where we are at a particular moment in time.

Symbolic Sign: "bear no resemblance to the objects to which they refer. The association is arbitrary and must be learned within the culture as a matter of convention" (Griffin et al., 2015, p. 336).

Pre-chorus: Reminding listeners that the chorus is coming up next: a feature particularly helpful to the people who only know the words to the chorus.

Section 4:

Dorian Mode: an ancient Greek mode represented on the white keys of the piano by a descending diatonic scale from D to D.

Fine Art: "a way of presenting that is purposive on its own and that furthers, even though without a purpose, the culture of our mental powers to [facilitate] social communication" (I. Kant, 1987, p.173).

Harmony: An agreement or a reconciliation of opposites, where two sides that are seemingly in disagreement, come together to produce a pleasing sound.

Katharsis: An effect of art that is the purgation or purification of emotions of pity and fear.

Lydian Mode: an ancient Greek mode represented on the white keys of the piano by a descending diatonic scale from F to F.

Mimesis: a concept that speaks of art as an imitation, reflection, or representation of the natural world.

Neo-Platonists: "A Neoplatonist believed, first, that the world perceived by our sense organs was only a grosser reflection of a realer world, God's world, that we perceive with our God-given capacity for reasoning; and, second, that the purest form of reasoning was numerical reasoning, because it was least limited to what our senses tell us" (Taruskin, 2005, p.1).

Phrygian Mode: "an ancient Greek mode represented on the white keys of the piano by a descending diatonic scale from E to E" (Merriam-Webster, 2020).

Sound (Boethius): "a percussion of the air which is undissolved even to the hearing" (Boethius, 1985, p.134).

Tragedy: A form of poetry that is "essentially an imitation not of persons but of action and life, of happiness and misery" (Aristotle, 2001, 1450a).

Section 5:

Politics: the system(s) of governance a society has developed to organize itself.

WORKS CITED:

Adams, N. (2013). The Inspiring Force Of 'We Shall Overcome' [article]. Retrieved from NPR website on July 7, 2020: https://www.npr.org/2013/08/28/216482943/the-inspiring-force-of-we-shall-overcome

Adorno. T. W. (2001). The Culture Industry: Selected Essays on Mass Culture. (J. M. Berstein, Trans.) New York, NY: Routledge Publishing.

Akatemia, S. (2011). Listening to music lights up the whole brain [article]. Retrieved from the AlphaGalileo website on July 31, 2020: https://www.alphagalileo.org/en-gb/Item-Display/ItemId/82891?returnurl=https://www.alphagalileo.org/en-gb/Item-Display/ItemId/82891

Aristotle., Edited, McKeon, R. (2001). The Basic Works of Aristotle. New York, NY: Random House Publishing Inc.

Arkenberg, R. (2002). Music in the Renaissance [article]. Retrieved from the Met Museum website on July 14, 2020: https://www.metmuseum.org/toah/hd/renm/hd_renm.htm

Augustine, St. (1964) De Musica Book VI. Albert Hofstadter, Richard Kuhns eds. Philosophies of Art and Beauty. Chicago, IL: University of Chicago Press. 185-202.

Augustine, St. (1997) The Confessions. M. Boulding, trans. New York, NY: Random House Publishing Inc.

AZ Lyrics (2020). Paperback Writer [song lyrics]. Retrieved from the AZ Lyrics website on August 1, 2020: https://www.azlyrics.com/lyrics/beatles/paperbackwriter.html

Bailey, D. T. J. (2005). Logic and Music in Plato's "Phaedo." Phronesis, 50(2), 95–115.

BBC Bitesize. (2020). Expressionism [article]. Retrieved from the BBC Bitesize website on July 20, 2020: https://www.bbc.co.uk/bitesize/guides/zxx3b9q/revision/1

BBC Music Magazine (2016). What is a String Quartet? [article]. Retrieved from the BBC Music Magazine website on July 20, 2020: https://www.classical-music.com/features/articles/what-string-quartet/

Beecham, T. (1959). A Mingled Chime. London, UK: Hutchinson.

Bennet II, J. (2017). How Many Movements are there in a Symphony? [article]. Retrieved from the WQXR website on July 22, 2020: https://www.wqxr.org/story/what-are-four-movements-symphony/

Bennett, J. (2015). How Was Musical Notation Invented? A Brief History. WQXR Public Radio. New York, NY.

Bereska, T. (2018). Deviance, Conformity, and Social Control in Canada [fifth ed]. Toronto, ON: Pearson Canada Inc.

Berger, M., Gray, J. A., & Roth, B. L. (2009). The Expanded Biology of Serotonin. Annual Review of Medicine, 60, 1-15. https://doi.org/10.1146/annurev.med.60.042307.110802

Bergland, C. (2014). Why do the songs from your past evoke such vivid memories? [article]. Retrieved from the Psychology Today website on July 31, 2020: https://www.psychologytoday.com/ca/blog/the-athletes-way/201312/why-do-the-songs-your-past-evoke-such-vivid-memories

Berkowitz, P. (ed.) (2003). Never a Matter of Indifference: Sustaining Virtue in a Free Republic. Stanford, CA: Hoover Institution Press.

Berry, K. D. (2017). Singing in Slavery: Songs of Survival, Songs of Freedom [article]. Retrieved from PBS website on July 4, 2020: http://www.pbs.org/mercy-street/blogs/mercy-street-revealed/songs-of-survival-and-songs-of-freedom-during-slavery/#:~:text=Music%20was%20a%20way%20for,known%20as%20%E2%80%9CNegro%20Spirituals%E2%80%9D.

Blakemore, E. (2018). How the Black Power Protest at the 1968 Olympics Killed Careers [article]. Retrieved from History website on August 5, 2020: https://www.history.com/news/1968-mexico-city-olympics-black-power-protest-backlash

Boethius, A. M. S. (1985). Five Books on Music (James Garceau, Kevin

Long, Susan Burnham, Michael Waldstein, Thomas McGovern, Trans.). Online. http://static1.squarespace.com/

Bottoroli, S., Rosi, A., Russo, R., Vecchi, T. & Cavallini, E. (2014). The cognitive effects of listening to background music on older adults: processing speed improves with upbeat music, while memory seems to benefit from both upbeat and downbeat music [academic article]. Retrieved from the Frontiers website on July 31, 2020: https://www. frontiersin.org/articles/10.3389/fnagi.2014.00284/full

Branch, T. (2013). The King Years: Historic Moments in the Civil Rights Movement. New York: Simon & Schuster.

Buelow G. J. (1993) Music and Society in the Late Baroque Era. In: Buelow G.J. (ed.) The Late Baroque Era. Man & Music. Palgrave Macmillan, London

Cambridge Dictionary (2020). Music [definition]. Retrieved from the Cambridge Dictionary website on July 9, 2020: https://dictionary. cambridge.org/dictionary/english/music

Chan, L., Livingstone, S. & Russo, F. (2013). Facial Mimicry in Response to Song [academic publication]. Retrieved from the University of California Press website on July 29, 2020: https://online.ucpress.edu/mp/article/30/4/361/62571/Facial-Mimicry-in-Response-to-Song

Chanda, M. L., & Levitin, D. J. (2013). The neurochemistry of music. Trends in Cognitive Sciences, 17(4), 179–193. https://doi.org/10.1016/j. tics.2013.02.007

Chapman, R.(2011). Culture Wars: An Encyclopedia of Issues, Viewpoints, and Voices. M.E. Sharpe.

Chow, A.R. (2020). The Hamilton Movie Is Finally Upon Us. But Is the Groundbreaking Musical Already Outdated [article]? Retrieved from Time website on July 3, 2020: https://time.com/5858556/hamilton-disney-plus/

Chukwuma, K., Gerber, E., Pistanska, T., Kim, D. & Kim, M. (2017). Identity through the eyes of music: music and identity in a globalized world [article]. Retrieved from the Diggit Blog website on August 1, 2020: https://www.diggitmagazine.com/blog/identity-through-eyes-music#:~:text=Music%20seems%20to%20be%20a,both%20self%20and%20the%20collective.&text=Music%20constructs%20our%20sense%20of,ourselves%20in%20imaginable%20cultural%20narratives.

Clark, A. (2019). How 'The Birth of a Nation' Revived the Ku Klux Klan [article]. Retrieved from History website on July 5, 2020: https://www.history.com/news/kkk-birth-of-a-nation-film

Clark, C. & Warren, J. (2015). Music, memory, and mechanisms in Alzheimer's disease [academic article]. Retrieved from the NCBI website on July 31, 2020: https://www.ncbi.nlm.nih.gov/pmc/articles/PMC4511859/

Classic FM. (2020). The Story behind the Rite of Spring [article]. Retrieved from the Classic FM website on July 26, 2020: https://www.classicfm.com/composers/stravinsky/guides/story-behind-rite-spring/

Claydon, S. (2018). The science behind why choir-singing is good for you [article]. Retrieved from CBC website: https://www.cbc.ca/radio/blogs/the-science-behind-why-choir-singing-is-good-for-you-1.4594292

Cone, J.H. (1991). Martin & Malcolm & America: A Dream or a Nightmare. New York: Orbis Books.

Dartmouth College (2005). Researchers find where musical memories are stored in the brain. Retrieved from the phys org website on July 31, 2020: https://phys.org/news/2005-03-musical-memories-brain.html#:~:text=March%209%2C%202005-,Researchers%20find%20where%20musical%20memories%20are%20stored%20in%20the%20brain,holds%20on%20to%20musical%20memories.

David, D. (2008). Olympic athletes who took a stand [article]. Retrieved from Smithsonian website on August 5, 2020: https://www.smithsonianmag.com/articles/olympic-athletes-who-took-a-stand-593920/

David, K.C. (2020). The History of Politics in the Olympic Games [article]. Retrieved from The Takeaway website on August 5, 2020: https://www.wnycstudios.org/podcasts/takeaway/segments/229889-history-politics-olympic-games

Dixon, D. (2015). A brief history on hip-hop [article]. Retrieved from Scalar on July 31, 2020: https://scalar.usc.edu/works/breakdancers-vocaloids-and-gamers-east-asian-youth-cultures-spring-2015/a-brief-history-on-hip-hop

Droog, L. (2020). Personal Communication. July 19, 2020.

Du Bois, W.E.B. (1935). Black Reconstruction in America: An Essay Toward a History of the Part Which Black Folk Played in the Attempt to Reconstruct Democracy in America, 1860-1880.

Du Noyer, P. (ed.) (2003). The Billboard Illustrated Encyclopedia of Music. Billboard Books, New York: NY

Elert, G. (2020). The Physics Hypertextbook [webpage]. Retrieved from the Physics.info website on July 7, 2020: https://physics.info/music/

Encyclopaedia Britannica (2020). Cadenza [definition]. Retrieved from the Encyclopaedia Britannica website on July 22, 2020: https://www.britannica.com/art/cadenza

Encyclopaedia Britannica (2020). Consonance and Dissonance [article]. Retrieved from the Encyclopaedia Britannica website on July 20, 2020: https://www.britannica.com/art/consonance-music

Encyclopaedia Britannica (2020). Emotion [definition]. Retrieved from the Encyclopaedia Britannica website on July 22, 2020: https://www.britannica.com/science/emotion

Encyclopaedia Britannica (2020). Gangsta rap [definition]. Retrieved from the Encyclopaedia Britannica website on August 1, 2020: https://www.britannica.com/art/gangsta-rap

Encyclopaedia Britannica (2020). Gigue[definition]. Retrieved from the Encyclopaedia Britannica website on July 14, 2020: https://www.britannica.com/art/gigue

Encyclopaedia Britannica (2020). History of Publishing [article]. Retrieved from the Encyclopaedia Britannica website on August 1, 2020:

https://www.britannica.com/topic/publishing/The-book-club

Encyclopaedia Britannica (2020). Impressionism [article]. Retrieved from the Encyclopaedia Britannica website on July 20, 2020: https://www.britannica.com/art/Impressionism-music

Encyclopaedia Britannica (2020). Lied [definition]. Retrieved from the Encyclopaedia Britannica website on July 20, 2020: https://www.britannica.com/art/lied

Encyclopaedia Britannica (2020). Musical Form [definition]. Retrieved from the Encyclopaedia Britannica website on July 7, 2020: https://www.britannica.com/art/musical-form

Encyclopaedia Britannica (2020). Organum [definition]. Retrieved from the Encyclopaedia Britannica website on July 14, 2020: https://www.britannica.com/art/organum

Encyclopaedia Britannica (2020). Pitch [definition]. Retrieved from the Encyclopaedia Britannica website on July 7, 2020: https://www.britannica.com/art/pitch-music

Encyclopaedia Britannica (2020). Program music [article]. Retrieved from the Encyclopaedia Britannica website on July 23, 2020: https://www.britannica.com/art/program-music

Encyclopaedia Britannica (2020). Psychology [definition]. Retrieved from the Encyclopaedia Britannica website on July 28, 2020: https://www.britannica.com/science/psychology

Encyclopaedia Britannica (2020). Romanticism Music [article]. Retrieved from the Encyclopaedia Britannica website on July 20, 2020: https://www.britannica.com/art/Romanticism/Music

Encyclopaedia Britannica (2020). Scherzo [definition]. Retrieved from the Encyclopaedia Britannica website on July 22, 2020: https://www.britannica.com/art/scherzo

Encyclopaedia Britannica (2020). Sonata Form [article]. Retrieved from the Encyclopaedia Britannica website on July 22, 2020: https://www.britannica.com/art/sonata-form

Encyclopaedia Britannica (2020). Tone [definition]. Retrieved from the Encyclopaedia Britannica website on July 7, 2020: https://www.britannica.com/science/tone-sound

Everett, W. (1993). Voice leading and harmony as expressive devices in the early music of the Beatles: She Loves You [article]. Retrieved from the College Music Symposium website on August 1, 2020: https://symposium.music.org/index.php/32/item/2089-voice-leading-and-harmony-as-expressive-devices-in-the-early-music-of-the-beatles-she-loves-you

Fedotin, J. (2018). Before Kaepernick: Mahmoud Abdul-Rauf Sacrificed NBA Career To Protest Injustice [article]. Retrieved from The Post Game website on July 9, 2020: http://www.thepostgame.com/mahmoud-abdul-rauf-big3-nba-kaepernick-anthem

Foner, E. (2014). Reconstruction: America's Unfinished Revolution, 1863-1877. New York, New York: HarperPerennial.
Gerbert, M. ed., (2005). De cantu et musica sacra, I, trans. R. Taruskin ,74.

Gilmore, M. (1990). Bob Dylan, the Beatles, and the Rock of the Sixties [article]. Retrieved from the Rolling Stone website on August 1, 2020: https://www.rollingstone.com/music/music-features/bob-dylan-the-beatles-and-the-rock-of-the-sixties-176221/

Gordon-Reed, A. (2016). The intense debates surrounding Hamilton don't diminish the musical—they enrich it [article]. Retrieved from Vox website on July 4, 2020: https://www.vox.com/the-big-idea/2016/9/13/12894934/hamilton-debates-history-race-politics-literature

Gracyk, T. A. (1992). Adorno, Jazz, and the Aesthetics of Popular Music. The Musical Quarterly, 76(4), 526–542. JSTOR.

Griffin, E., Ledbetter, A., & Sparks, G. (2015). A First Look at Communication Theory [ninth edition]. New York, NY: McGraw-Hill Education.

Henschel, J. Personal communication. July 31, 2020.

History.com (2020). America meets the Beatles on "The Ed Sullivan Show" [article]. Retrieved from the History.com website on August 1, 2020: https://www.history.com/this-day-in-history/america-meets-the-beatles-on-the-ed-sullivan-show

History.com editors. (2019). Francis Scott Key pens "The Star-Spangled Banner" [article]. Retrieved from History website on July 8, 2020: https://www.history.com/this-day-in-history/key-pens-star-spangled-banner#:~:text=On%20September%2014%2C%201814%2C%20Francis,during%20the%20War%20of%201812

Hollis, B. (2017). Physics of Sound [article]. Retrieved from The Method Behind the Music website on July 7, 2020: https://method-behind-the-music.com/mechanics/physics/

Hurlemann, R., Patin, A., Onur, O. A., Cohen, M. X., Baumgartner, T., Metzler, S., ... Kendrick, K. M. (2010). Oxytocin Enhances Amygdala-Dependent, Socially Reinforced Learning and Emotional Empathy in Humans. Journal of Neuroscience, 30(14), 4999–5007. https://doi.org/10.1523/JNEUROSCI.5538-09.2010

Jakobson, R. (1963). Essais de linguistique générale. Paris, France: Minuit.

Jenkins, T. (2014). Why does music evoke memories? [article]. Retrieved from the BBC News website on July 31, 2020: https://www.bbc.com/culture/article/20140417-why-does-music-evoke-memories

Jhain, S. (2020). Evolution of the Beatles: visualizing how the band's music evolved overtime [webpage]. Retrieved from Sambhav Jain's website on August 1, 2020: https://www.sambhav-jain.com/beatles#:~:text=Rooted%20in%20skiffle%2C%20beat%2C%20and,recording%20techniques%20in%20innovative%20ways.

Jukely, T. (2018). Who started rap? A brief summary on the history of rap and hip-hop [article]. Retrieved from Four Over Four on July 31, 2020: https://www.fouroverfour.jukely.com/culture/history-of-rap-hip-hop/

Juslin, P. & Laukka, P. (2010). Expression, Perception, and Induction of Musical Emotions: A Review and a Questionnaire Study of Everyday Listening [academic article]. Journal of New Music Research 33(3) p. 217

- 238. DOI:10.1080/0929821042000317813

Kant, I. (1987). Critique of Judgement (W. S. Pluhar, Trans.). Indianapolis, IN: Hackett Publishing Company.

Kendi, I. X. (2016). Stamped from the beginning: The definitive history of racist ideas in America. New York: Nation Books.

Kerman, J. & Tomlinson, G. (2015). Listen (8th edition). W. W. Norton & Company Inc, New York: NY

Khan Academy (2020). Standing Waves Review [article]. Retrieved from the Khan Academy website in July 7, 2020: https://www.khanacademy.org/science/ap-physics-1/ap-mechanical-waves-and-sound/standing-waves-ap/a/standing-waves-review-ap

Lane, A., Luminet, O., Rimé, B., Gross, J. J., Timary, P. de, & Mikolajczak, M. (2013). Oxytocin increases willingness to socially share one's emotions. International Journal of Psychology, 48(4), 676–681. https://doi.org/10.1080/00207594.2012.677540

Largent, K. J. (n.d.). Harriet Beecher Stowe: The little woman who wrote the book that started this great war [article]. Retrieved from eHistory website on August 3, 2020: https://ehistory.osu.edu/articles/harriet-beecher-stowe-little-woman-who-wrote-book-started-great-war

LedgerNote (2020). Musical Key Characteristics & Emotions [article]. Retrieved from the LedgerNote website on July 30, 2020: https://ledgernote.com/blog/interesting/musical-key-characteristics-emotions/#:~:text=E%20Minor&text=This%20key%20can%20carry%20grief%2C%20mournfulness%2C%20restlessness.

Levitan, D. J. (2006). This Is Your Brain on Music: The Science of a Human Obsession. Penguin Group Inc. New York, New York.
Lewisohn, M. (1988). The Beatles Recording Sessions. New York, NY: Harmony Books.

Lineberry, C. (2007). The Story Behind the Star Spangled Banner [article]. Retrieved from Smithsonian website on July 8, 2020: https://www.smithsonianmag.com/history/the-story-behind-the-star-spangled-banner-149220970/

Loui, P. & Wessel, D. (2007). Harmonic expectation and affect in Western music: Effects of attention and training. 69(7) pp. 1084 - 1092.

Lumen Learning (2020). Renaissance Music [article]. Retrieved from the Lumen Learning website on July 14, 2020: https://courses.lumenlearning. com/musicappreciation_with_theory/chapter/renaissance-music/

Lumen Learning (2020). Schubert: Der Erlkonig [article]. Retrieved from the Lumen Learning website on July 29, 2020: https:// courses.lumenlearning.com/musicapp_historical/chapter/der-erlkonig/#:~:text=It%20depicts%20the%20death%20of,1782%20 Singspiel%20entitled%20Die%20Fischerin.

Marazziti, D., Dell'Osso, B., Baroni, S., Mungai, F., Catena, M., Rucci, P., ... Dell'Osso, L. (2006). A relationship between oxytocin and anxiety of romantic attachment. Clinical Practice and Epidemiology in Mental Health, 6.

McIntosh, J. (2018) What is serotonin and what does it do? Reviewed by D. R. Wilson. [article]. Retrieved from Medical News Today website: https://www.medicalnewstoday.com/articles/232248

Medical Biochemistry. (n.d.). Biochemistry of nerve transmission [article]. Retrieved from the Medical Biochemistry Page website on July 14, 2020: http://themedicalbiochemistrypage.org/biochemistry-of-nerve-transmission/#5ht

Menon, V., & Levitin, D. J. (2005). The rewards of music listening: Response and physiological connectivity of the mesolimbic system. NeuroImage, 28(1), 175–184. https://doi.org/10.1016/j.neuroimage.2005.05.053

Merriam-Webster (2020). Troubadour [definition]. Retrieved from the Merriam-Webster website on July 13, 2020: https://www.merriam-webster.com/dictionary/troubadour

Merriam-Webster Dictionary. (2020) "Muse" [dictionary entry]. https:// www.merriam-webster.com/dictionary/muse

Monteiro, L. (2016). Race-Conscious Casting and the Erasure of the Black Past in Lin-Manuel Miranda's Hamilton. The Public Historian, 38(1), 89-98. doi:10.2307/26420757

Moraes, M. M., Rabelo, P. C. R., Pinto, V. A., Pires, W., Wanner, S. P., Szawka, R. E., & Soares, D. D. (2018). Auditory stimulation by exposure to melodic music increases dopamine and serotonin activities in rat forebrain areas linked to reward and motor control. Neuroscience Letters, 673, 73–78. https://doi.org/10.1016/j.neulet.2018.02.058

Moreira, S., Justi, F. & Moreira, M. (2018). Can musical intervention improve memory in Alzheimer's patients? Evidence from a systematic review. Dement Neuropsychol 12(2) p. 133 - 142.

MyHealth Alberta. (2018). Harmful Noise Levels [chart]. Retrieved from the MyHealth Alberta website on July 5, 2020: https://myhealth.alberta.ca/Health/Pages/conditions.aspx?hwid=tf4173

MyTutor. (2019). What is a Ritornello Form? Retrieved from MyTutor UK website on July 22, 2020: https://www.mytutor.co.uk/answers/19571/GCSE/Music/What-is-a-ritornello-form/

Nichols, A. (2016). You Should Be Terrified That People Who Like "Hamilton" Run Our Country [article]. Retrieved from Current Affairs website on July 3, 2020: https://www.currentaffairs.org/2016/07/you-should-be-terrified-that-people-who-like-hamilton-run-our-country

Nilsson, U. (2009). Soothing music can increase oxytocin levels during bed rest after open-heart surgery: A randomised control trial. Journal of Clinical Nursing, 18(15), 2153–2161. https://doi.org/10.1111/j.1365-2702.2008.02718.x

Open Music Theory (2018). Minuet Form [article]. Retrieved from the Open Music Theory website on July 22, 2020: http://openmusictheory.com/minuet.html

Papas, S. (2015). Oxytocin: Facts About the "Cuddle Hormone" [article]. Retrieved from Livescience website on July 14, 2020: https://www.livescience.com/42198-what-is-oxytocin.html

Parncutt, R. (2014). The emotional connotations of major versus minor tonality: One or more origins? [research abstract]. Retrieved from the Sagepub website on July 30, 2020: https://journals.sagepub.com/doi/10.1177/1029864914542842

PBS. (2009). Interview with Daniel Levitin - Part One Music Instinct [interview]. Retrieved from PBS website: https://www.pbs.org/wnet/musicinstinct/mi-blog/interview/interview-with-daniel-levitin-part-1/18/ PBS. (n.d.). Conditions of antebellum slavery [article]. Retrieved from PBS website on July 4, 2020: https://www.pbs.org/wgbh/aia/part4/4p2956.html

PBS (2020). Berlioz's Symphonie Fantastique. Retrieved from the PBS website on July 30, 2020: https://www.pbs.org/keepingscore/berlioz-symphonie-fantastique.html

Pearce, M. & Wiggins, G. (2012). Auditory expectation: the information dynamics of music perception and cognition. Retrieved from the Wiley Online Library on July 11, 2020: https://onlinelibrary.wiley.com/doi/full/10.1111/j.1756-8765.2012.01214.x

Plato., trans. Cornford, F. M. (1945). The Republic of Plato. London ; New York: Oxford University Press.

Plato., trans. Denyer, N. (2008). Protagoras. Cambridge: UK, Cambridge University Press,

Pouska, A. (2020). Keys in Music [webpage]. Retrieved from the Study Bass website on July 30, 2020: https://www.studybass.com/lessons/harmony/keys-in-music/

Reed, I. (2015). "Hamilton: the Musical:" Black Actors Dress Up like Slave Traders...and It's Not Halloween [article]. Retrieved from counterpunch website on July 3, 2020: https://www.counterpunch.org/2015/08/21/hamilton-the-musical-black-actors-dress-up-like-slave-tradersand-its-not-halloween/

Ribero, F., Santos, F., Albuquerque, P. & Oliveira-Silva, P. (2019). Emotional Induction Through Music: Measuring Cardiac and Electrodermal Responses of Emotional States and Their Persistence [article]. Retrieved from the Frontiers in Psychology website on July 29, 2020: https://www.frontiersin.org/articles/10.3389/fpsyg.2019.00451/full

Robin, W. (2016). Colin Kaepernick and the radical uses of the "Star Spangled Banner." [article]. Retrieved from the New Yorker Website on July 9, 2020: https://www.newyorker.com/culture/culture-desk/colin-kaepernick-and-the-radical-uses-of-the-star-spangled-banner

Romano, A. (2020). Why Hamilton is as frustrating as it is brilliant — and impossible to pin down [article]. Retrieved from Vox website on July 4, 2020: https://www.vox.com/culture/21305967/hamilton-debate-controversy-historical-accuracy-explained

Salamon, M. (2013). 11 Interesting Effects of Oxytocin [article]. Retrieved from Livescience website on July 14, 2020: https://www.livescience.com/35219-11-effects-of-oxytocin.html

Salimpoor, V. N., Benovoy, M., Larcher, K., Dagher, A., & Zatorre, R. J. (2011). Anatomically distinct dopamine release during anticipation and experience of peak emotion to music. Nature Neuroscience, 14(2), 257–262. https://doi.org/10.1038/nn.2726

Scarinci, D. (2017). 1943 Court Ruling Offers Insight on National Anthem Controversy [article]. Retrieved from The Observer website on July 7, 2020: https://observer.com/2017/11/1943-court-ruling-offers-insight-on-national-anthem-controversy/

Schaeffer, P., North, C., & Dack, J. (2017). Treatise on Musical Objects : An Essay Across Disciplines. University of California Press.

Schopenhauer, A. (1969). The World as Will and Representation (E. F. J. Payne, Trans.). New York, NY: Dover Publications Inc.

Scruton, R. (2009). Understanding Music: Philosophy and Interpretation. London, UK: Continuum.

Sehyan, A. (2009). What is Romanticism and where did it come from? [article]. Retrieved from the Cambridge University Press website on July 26, 2020: https://www.cambridge.org/core/books/cambridge-companion-to-german-romanticism/what-is-romanticism-and-where-did-it-

come-from/884CEB14F83E3443A148DBC4B77B6617#:~:text=The%20
etymology%20of%20the%20word,which%20were%20developed%20
from%20Latin.

Simon, H. B. (2015). Music as Medicine. The American Journal of Medicine, 128(2), 208–210. https://doi.org/10.1016/j.amjmed.2014.10.023

Smithsonian. (n.d.). Roots of African American Music [article]. Retrieved from Smithsonian website on July 4, 2020: https://www.si.edu/spotlight/african-american-music/roots-of-african-american-music

Smith-Strickland, K. (2015). There Actually is Sound in Outer Space [article]. Retrieved from the Gizmodo website on July 3, 2020: https://gizmodo.com/there-actually-is-sound-in-outer-space-1738420340

Somara, S. (2016). The Physics of Music: Crash Course Physics #19 [video]. Retrieved from the Crash Course YouTube Channel on July 7, 2020: https://www.youtube.com/watch?v=XDsk6tZX55g

Stoller, M. (2017). The Hamilton Hustle [article]. Retrieved on July 3, 2020: https://thebaffler.com/salvos/hamilton-hustle-stoller

Tarasti, E. (2018). Musical Semiotics - a Discipline, its History and Theories, Past and Present [article]. Retrieved from the Erudit website on July 27, 2020: https://www.erudit.org/en/journals/rssi/2016-v36-n3-rssi03971/1051395ar/#:~:text=In%20its%20actual%20form%20musical,and%20popular%20forms%20of%20music.

Taruskin, R. (2005). "Chapter 2: New Styles and Forms" [Book chapter]. In Oxford University Press, Music from the Earliest Notations to the Sixteenth Century. New York, USA.

Taruskin, R. (2005). "Chapter 3: Retheorizing Music" [Book chapter]. Oxford University Press, Music from the Earliest Notations to the Sixteenth Century. New York, USA.

Taruskin, R. (2005) The Oxford History of Western Music. Oxford, England: Oxford University Press.

Taylor & Francis. (2013). Music brings memories back to the injured brain. [article]. Retrieved from the Science Daily website on July 31, 2020: https://www.sciencedaily.com/releases/2013/12/131210072030.htm

Texas v. Johnson, 491 U.S. 397 (1989)

The Beatles Bible (2020). Paperback Writer [webpage]. Retrieved from the Beatles Bible website on August 1, 2020: https://www.beatlesbible. com/songs/paperback-writer/

Toobin, J. (2016). Colin Kaepernick and a Landmark Supreme Court Case [article]. Retrieved from the New Yorker website on July 9, 2020: https://www.newyorker.com/news/daily-comment/colin-kaepernick-and-a-landmark-supreme-court-case

Toor, A. (2013). 100 years ago today, 'The Rite of Spring' incited a riot in a Paris theatre [article]. Retrieved from The Verge website on July 26, 2020: https://www.theverge.com/2013/5/29/4375736/igor-stravinsky-rite-of-spring-100-anniversary-paris-riot

Torrance, R. (2019). What is a Concerto Grosso? Retrieved from the ABC Classic website on July 19, 2020: https://www.abc.net.au/classic/read-and-watch/music-reads/what-is-a-concerto-grosso/11749364

Turner, S. (2018). The Complete Beatles Songs: the stories behind every track written by the fab four [second edition]. London, UK: Carlon Books Limited.
Viagas, R. (2015). Hamilton Confirms Whopping $57 Million Advance Sale [article]. Retrieved from Playbill website on July 3, 2020: https:// www.playbill.com/article/hamilton-confirms-whopping-57-million-advance-sale-com-370831

Vozick-Levinson, S. (2015). Revolution on Broadway: Inside Hip-Hop History Musical 'Hamilton' [article]. Retrieved from Rolling Stone website on July 3, 2020: https://www.rollingstone.com/culture/culture-features/revolution-on-broadway-inside-hip-hop-history-musical-hamilton-74059/

Washington, J. (2016). Still no anthem, still no regrets for Mahmoud Abdul-Rauf [article]. Retrieved from Undefeated website on July 9, 2020: https://theundefeated.com/features/abdul-rauf-doesnt-regret-sitting-out-national-anthem/

Western Michigan University (n.d.). Modern Art Music [webpage]. Retrieved from the Western Michigan University website on July 20, 2020: https://wmich.edu/mus-gened/mus150/1500%20webbook%20 modern%20artmusic/Modern%20ArtMusic.htm

West Virginia State Bd. of Educ. v. Barnette, 319 U.S. 624 (1943)

Witkin, R. W. (2000). Why did Adorno "Hate" Jazz? Sociological Theory, 18(1), 145–170. JSTOR.

Young, D. & Stadler, S. (2018). Cutnell & Johnson Physics (11th edition). John Wiley & Sons Inc, Hoboken, NJ.

Younge, G. (2020). The man who raised a black power salute at the 1968 Olympic Games [interview]. Retrieved from The Guardian website on August 5, 2020: https://www.theguardian.com/world/2012/mar/30/black-power-salute-1968-olympics

Zatorre, R. J., & Halpern, A. R. (2005). Mental Concerts: Musical Imagery and Auditory Cortex. Neuron, 47(1), 9–12. https://doi.org/10.1016/j. neuron.2005.06.013